About the Author

Robert Noble Graham had a career in the oil, publishing and finance industries. He is a graduate in French and German and in English. He is divorced with two adult children, both scientists. He has written drama that has been produced on BBC Radio 4 and in Scottish theatres. He has contributed specialist financial articles to various journals and is a regular contributor to Mensa magazine. He lives in Scotland and is the author of travel books and novels:

By The Same Author

Novels

- MASKS OF VENICE
- THE CELEBRITY OF ANDERS HECHT
- THE WOMEN FROM CRETE

Travel Books

- COFFEE IN CUBA
- COFFEE, CASTANETS AND DON QUIXOTE
- COFFEE, CHIANTI AND CARAVAGGIO

All of the above are available either as e-books or print books.

ACKNOWLEDGEMENT

I am very grateful to Kristopher Krug. His knowledge of IT systems and his creativity have been invaluable in preparing the cover for this book

COFFEE WITH THE COLOSSUS

Giants of Greece

By

ROBERT NOBLE GRAHAM

Copyright February 2013

www.rngnovels.co.uk

CONTENTS

INTRODUCTION

COFFEE WITH THE COLOSSUS

The title of this volume might seem odd." Only Rhodes
had a Colossus", you might well say. The fact that two of
the book`s chapters deal with this wonderful island might
not seem a proper justification. The Colossus of Rhodes
was one of The Seven Wonders of the Ancient World.
However, the more I have travelled in Greece the more I
have felt the term applies to much more than that one
ancient figure on an island. Greece is a small country, but
its place in human history is immense. If you visit the
northern province of Epirus you are surrounded by high
mountains in the wild summits of which you find no fewer
than three dragon lakes, silent stretches where the
legendary creatures famously reside. You find more
gigantic mountains in Crete along with a uniquely huge
footprint on the history of the Eastern Mediterranean.
From there you can travel to the small island of Santorini
which was, however, the site of the most immense
volcanic explosion in recorded history. Then there is
Rhodes itself. Nothing of the famous Colossus now
remains but the legend goes on and the island, like Crete,

has left a very large mark on history. Culturally, of course, that small area of what we now call Greece produced mathematicians, philosophers, dramatists, poets, doctors, historians, sculptors, myths and legends which have been the foundation of western culture and civilisation. Our direct debt to the Greece of more than 2,000 years ago is in itself colossal. If we add to that its indirect influence through the Romans, the Persians, the Turks and the Islamic scholars of the late Dark Ages it is greater still. If we measured cultural footprints as we are now encouraged to do with carbon ones Greece is perhaps the mightiest colossus in history.

As with its near neighbour, Egypt, you cannot help wondering what happened to that fountain of genius and accomplishment. Since its defeat at the hands of the Romans Greece seems to have contributed very little to the world other than a lot of olive oil and a huge merchant shipping fleet. Throughout this book I make reference to the various troubles the country has had but I haven't attempted to trace all that has brought it low. Most of it can be summed up by observing that it has not been very fortunate in its choice of neighbours. In recent years you could also note it has been equally unlucky in its choice of political leaders. Despite this, it has become a favourite holiday destination for a number of reasons. It has a lot of sunshine, beautiful and varied landscape and very good food. It has wine which may not delight very rich connoisseurs but is nonetheless most acceptable. Its people are, generally, very friendly, welcoming and humorous. I have now visited it many times and am fortunate to have made some good Greek friends. I have no doubt that I will write more about the country and its islands. I have kept this first book about it relatively brief. Although there is certainly the material to do it I didn`t want this publication to be another Colossus.

MY FIRST VISIT TO RHODES

Rhodes was the first of the Greek islands I visited. Quite late in life I formed the notion that I should like to see all of them before I die. It was only later I decided it might be wise to find out how many there were to see what size of task I had set myself. Books vary in their assessment between 1,400 and 3,000. This seemed like a lot and I decided I had to trim my ambitions. It was obviously sensible to ignore all the uninhabited ones, many of which are not much more than rocks in the sea. Then I decided to forget those only inhabited by goats and monks. That was a surprising number. When I then excluded ones inhabited by goats or monks that reduced it still further.

I began with Rhodes for a number of reasons. The primary one was that I could fly there direct from Glasgow at a time that suited me. I had decided to use a tour company called Solo`s which organises holidays for people without partners or whose partners do not want to holiday with them (more common than you would think). I had done various trips entirely on my own since the end of my marriage and I didn`t mind doing it. The freedom appealed to me but I had to admit that the evenings would have been improved by some company to discuss the day`s events. Solo`s offered a viable alternative: company if you wanted it, solitude if you preferred. They also had some attractive excursions on offer. I worried a little that I would be spending a week with some sad people, but that turned out not to be the case.

Our hotel was in Ialysos, a small town just a couple of miles south of the capital city, Rhodes Town, famous as what I thought had been the chosen location for the Knights Templar after the Muslims threw them out of Jerusalem. You will see later in the book that this belief was not quite correct. The Knights Templar have, of course, become the stuff of much fact and fancy down the years and no wonder. Almost everything about them is entirely bizarre. They are thought to have formed an order to protect the Temple of Solomon (hence the name Templar) in Jerusalem. This was located on Temple Mount where Muslims erected the Al-Aqsa mosque. It was also allegedly the site of other events such as Abraham's encounter with the angel and the ascent of Mahomet into Heaven. The pseudo or real sacred associations pile up as you investigate and it has been described as the holiest place on earth. Considering the fighting and bloodshed that has surrounded it you could just as convincingly consider it the most bloodthirsty and godless. In any event, once the Muslims retook Jerusalem the Knights had to base themselves elsewhere and Rhodes was the chosen location.

After settling into a bright, comfortable modern hotel overlooking the sea (Aegean I think but one sea seamlessly merges into another in this part of the globe and they`re all part of the Mediterranean) at Ialysos we were invited to a reception where we met our rep and Jimmy the Greek. Our rep was an amazing fellow called Andrew. At first sight the only amazing thing about him was his suntan. He looked as if he`d been fired in an oven. As the week wore on we discovered he was a man of unusual stamina who could drink with the boys in town until 3 in the morning and still turn up for a hearty breakfast before most of us had stirred. Andrew gave us a brief rundown of the attractions of the island: the Venetian Harbour and Templar city in Rhodes town, the Butterfly Farm at Tholos, the citadel at Lindos, and the romantic ruined city of Kamiros. He innocently devastated one of our party who asked if there would be an excursion to see the Colossus since she had been saving for years to come and photograph it, having consistently failed to find pictures of it. Andrew gently explained that she was 2,296 years too late since the amazing 30 metre statue had only stood for 56 years before being destroyed by an earthquake. We have a high regard for the ancient Greeks and their intelligence but the thinking behind erecting a giant statue in iron and bronze in one of the world`s most active earthquake zones is not immediately clear. Her reaction suggested she suspected Andrew of malicious time travel to dismantle the Colossus to spite her, although he had never previously heard of her.

Then it was the turn of Jimmy the Greek. His name puzzled us a little. How many Greeks are called Jimmy and why did they need to tell us he was Greek since everyone else in the hotel also was? We were, after all, in Greece. He limped onto the stage on a pair of crutches, result evidently of taking a walk to buy a paper. He didn`t explain any further but perhaps a quick earthquake had got him. He was a stout fellow with amazingly heavy eyelids and a fleshy mouth. His job was to sell the excursions. He described the outings to Lindos and Kamiros in extravagant terms, but saved his Homeric gifts for the voyage to the little island of Symi. At this his eyes became misty and his voice seemed to break a little. He told us that the front at Symi was wonderfully beautiful but the real jewel of the island was the monastery of St. Michael on the other side from the capital. With pauses to deal with the emotional waves he told us that St. Michael`s spirit still presided over the lovely monastery and many well attested miracles had taken place there. "St. Michael will never let you down," he intoned. "When you are there ask him anything, anything, and then be prepared to be astonished." Nobody had the nerve to ask him "So, why are you still limping, Jimmy" but we did all wonder how many fridges he had sold to Lappland.

This visit was not long after I had begun to learn modern Greek. I really had no idea when I began what a difficult language it is. This fact draws a mixture of amusement, admiration and pity from Greeks. Since many of them speak acceptable English it`s not obvious to them why anyone would bother to learn their language which even exasperates them with its oddities and complications. However, my small and really rather unimpressive achievements in this regard entertained them greatly. Its benefits became quickly clear.

 There was no excursion available on our first day so I walked the two miles into Rhodes Town. The road skirted the sea and I walked beneath a bright blue sky with the sun not quite at its hottest. That eventually led me onto a beach which was at the southern end of the modern town. On sighting shops and restaurants I recognised that my caffeine levels were getting dangerously low. There were several cafés along the front. Greek cafés in my experience vary between the traditional ones, often referred to as kafeneios, where old men sit for most of the day smoking, and impressively modern ones with colourful, well upholstered sofas or minimalist high stools. I was very warm from my walk and the temptation to find the coolest shady corner was strong. However, I love looking out to blue skies and sea. I chose a café with small, neat leather chairs and little tables. I settled at one in the shade, still in sight of the beach. The cafe was quiet but soon a young woman with shoulder length blond hair curling round her ears and neck came over. She was a little fleshy but shapely. Her smile was natural and welcoming. I managed to greet her in her own language which drew a little smile. As I then proceeded to order my coffee in Greek her smile widened. "Bravo," she said in English, suggesting she was not overly impressed. "You are learning Greek. Why are you doing that?" I told her that languages interest me and Greek seemed like a challenge. She nodded as if she didn`t quite believe me, served me coffee and then refused payment for it.

I went on to find the historic town. I approached the impressive entrance gate with interest and anticipation. Most of the building dates from the 14th century when the knights moved in. They remained for two hundred years before the Turks drove them out. The Avenue of the Knights which consists of `inns` devoted to each of the seven countries that offered manpower remains a very impressive street, now largely occupied by offices. I went on from there to see the rest of the old town which was in excellent condition and suggested a group of men with taste in architecture and a fair grasp of how to live well. The weather in Rhodes is beautiful. There would have been ample wine, fruit, fish and olives. Perhaps not difficult to see why young men might have abandoned some of the pestilential slums of mediaeval Europe on a wet November afternoon for this. I left with the firm intention of discovering more about these enigmatic knights. However, the abundance of sheer nonsense written about them deterred me for a long time from carrying that out.

We then had our first excursion, a coach trip to some of the main sights of the island. Our guide was to be a very lovely young Athenian named Anne Marie whose mastery of English impressed me all the more when I learned she had never visited an English speaking country. We went first of all to Kamiros which was once the principal town of the island. It was largely destroyed by earthquakes in the third and second centuries B.C but the ruins still give a clear idea of the layout. It sits on the western coast on a gentle slope running down to the sea. As always in old Greek towns, the highest point is occupied by the temple or Acropolis, which means 'the top of the town'. From there it runs down almost to the coast, a neatly laid out town where shops, markets and fine houses all once existed. Anne Marie gave us a lucid account of its construction and what life must have been like. This was not altogether easy since one of our party was a round Glaswegian (I am also Glaswegian) with a voice several octaves below basso profundo and a tendency to relate the world to parts of Glasgow. He interrupted our guide with a question: "That street looks like one in Maryhill that goes down to the railway. Would they have had a railway?" Anne Marie hesitated for a moment, almost imperceptibly, as she wondered whether this might be some form of alien humour. One look at the furrowed brow and the blank eyes confirmed that he wasn`t joking. Gently, she pointed out that this had been built almost three thousand years before the first steam engine and even today there were no railways on Rhodes. He seemed to have a follow-up question but mercifully one of the women inquired about the Greek language and whether it had three genders. Anne-Marie confirmed it had but explained they were not always logical since the normal word for a dog was usually neuter. Our Glaswegian saw his chance and rumbled "Why did they neuter their dogs then? "

We travelled from there through very green countryside to Petaloudes or Butterfly Valley, This is a delightfully shaded, wooded area by a stream. In fact it has no butterflies at all but is a major breeding site for the Panaxaria moth. It was simply decided that `butterfly` sounds more endearing and less spooky than `moth` and anyway, even the one biologist in our group was not at all sure what the difference is. Sadly the moths are in steep decline for a strange reason. The adult moth has no stomach. It only survives by the energy it built up as a caterpillar. The large number of visitors disturbs them and makes them fly around more than they should, using up their scarce reserves. The valley was cool and still. Even without stomachs the moths, I felt, had taste.

From there we went up Mount Attavyros which, at 1215 metres is the island`s highest peak. We didn`t go to the summit but stopped at the town of Embonas, the hub of Rhodes` wine-growing area. Anne- Marie, like guides I had come across throughout southern Europe, was adept at reciting the advantages of the local produce. I don`t have a very discriminating palate for wine and I certainly never feel like drinking it in the late morning so I can`t really say how good it was. As always on these occasions, the bus emptied as if snakes had appeared on it and infirm ladies who had climbed aboard with difficulty showed impressive speed to join the queue. Busy as Anne-Marie appeared to be, our Glaswegian felt she would benefit from the knowledge that: "we make whisky in Scotland and you get different whisky in Islay from what you get on the Spey...." Martin, a quiet but pleasant London truck driver advised me that the red Cava Emery was a good choice. Evidently wine was a hobby of his. He and his mates often went to wine tastings so he apparently knew a bit about it. "Ye see, the difference is the water..." I heard my fellow Glaswegian intone with, as far as I could tell, no one listening.

Jimmy the Greek returned to our hotel that evening, still, apparently, being ignored by St. Michael. One of the other subjects about which he became emotional was "the completely unfair reputation given to Faliraki". It was true that most of us had heard it was the one place on the island that should be avoided unless you are an alcoholic teenager who doesn`t mind being assaulted, or waking up with  one or more people you can`t name and may not even like. Jimmy alleged that this reputation had come from one misinformed TV programme. We doubted that. However, he prevailed upon the more credulous of us to go along to `a wonderful restaurant ` in the town so we could appreciate how beautiful and friendly it is. In fact the restaurant was good and friendly, but on the way back one of the ladies had her handbag stolen and another was narrowly missed by a flying bottle. The lady got her handbag back when we all set off in pursuit of the culprit who, I feel, overrated the sprinting power of our party and abandoned the goods. Sadly, as with everything else we`d heard about the town`s shortcomings, the fellow was British.

The last excursion was to the delightful, tiny island of Symi. Symi is far nearer the Turkish coast than anything Greek and it is one of these anomalies of political history that Greece owns it. Most of us took this trip; several hoping St. Michael was good with hangovers. In fact the monastery was beautiful and impressive. Some people lingered, possibly with a long list for the saint. I noticed there was a tiny café attached, overlooking the sea. After appreciating the fine building and its atmosphere I decided to enjoy the sunshine. Two ladies served. One was a quiet but smiling dark-haired woman. The other was a severe looking older one. I thought I`d make her day by ordering in Greek. She glared at me silently for a moment and then said "What are you wanting?" in a tone that suggested working so close to a holy place was a strain on the nerves. I said "coffee" but before I managed to define whether I wanted espresso, Americano, latte, skinny latte, mocha or any other variation she splashed boiling water into a mug with a sprinkling of Nescafe at the bottom. She then squirted some evaporated milk into it and glared at me again in a "well are you going to pay me or do I have to take hostile action?" type of manner. I handed over a euro and retreated to the sunshine, wondering if Michael could manage a quick thunderbolt.

After an hour at the monastery the boat took us round to the town for lunch. The bay was as picturesque as in most of these Greek islands and mainland harbours. Houses in orange, pink, blue and white all clustered merrily at the front and open air restaurants bustled with trade. Andrew led us to one where we sat at two long tables. The waiter, whom I took also to be the owner, chatted smilingly to us, glad to explain the menu in very acceptable English. He was around forty, I guessed, a little overweight but with the right kind of easy but efficient manner. I always like to try menu items which I have never tasted before so when I saw `sea snails` as an option I thought that would be interesting. "No, don`t take them," instructed the waiter. I was surprised. "Why not?" "Because you won`t like them"

18

"How do you know?" I questioned. "Nobody does," he replied. It occurred to me to ask why they were on offer at all, but decided not to pursue it. Maybe he served them as a treat to customers he didn`t want to see again.

My week on Rhodes was excellent. I liked the island very much and felt that it would be well worth a return visit before too long. That took a few years but it happened as you will see later.

CRETE – THE FIRST VISIT

I made my first trip to the largest of the Greek islands with my friend, Suzie. We had booked rooms at a hotel in Stalis (or Stalithas) This settlement is about 30 kilometres or 19 miles east of the capital, Heraklion, so it was a good base from which to visit the wonderful site of Knossos. It was also convenient for travelling further east to Agia Nikolaos, Elounda and the sad but fascinating island of Spinalonga, the site of the last leper colony in Europe. Stalis forms part of an almost uninterrupted coastal development from Hersonissos round to Malia, but, unlike these two, has not mushroomed around nightclubs and bars. Our apartment was a short walk from the main road, but our balcony looked straight out over the Bay of Malia, a calm inlet from the Sea of Crete. We could sit on our balcony in the morning at a first cup of tea and watch the sun rise and see it light up the high hills to the east before becoming uncomfortably hot.

If you are in suitably reverent mood Stalis is well positioned for a short taxi ride to Dikteon Cave just outside the village of Psyhro. The importance of this cave in cosmic history is that it was the birthplace of Zeus, mighty king of the gods, who presided over the unruly deities who created mayhem at the Trojan War and throughout the wonderful but disturbing Greek tragedies. Almost all of the Hellenic myths record Crete as his birthplace although he later migrated to Mount Olympos on the Greek mainland. Zeus also sired countless children in various improbable forms such as that of a large bull, the form in which he is said to have raped Europa. The cult of the bull was powerful in Crete, as witnessed by the Minotaur myth. The origin of the name `Europa` looks like two ancient Greek words meaning `broad` and `face`, possibly suggesting a cow. Their coupling simply looks like an old fertility myth. In something like human form he took up residence on Olympus where he tried to control the unruly gods   and fired colossal thunderbolts at moments of transcendental tedium. His mother, Rhea, sheltered the tiny Zeus in the Dikteon cave to save him from his father, Cronos, who liked to eat up his offspring. There is a startlingly vivid representation of this flawed parent by Goya as "Saturn devouring his children". This was one of the 14 nightmare paintings the great Spanish artist created and hung in his house *Quinta del Sordo* (House of the Deaf Man). It can now be seen in the Prado in Madrid by anyone in need of a really bad dream. There was great confusion between the ancient titan Cronos and the god Chronos, the god of time (hence chronology) whose Roman counterpart is Saturn. This simply sums up the indisputable fact that time brings all things into being and ensures their destruction. When Zeus grew up he put an end to his father`s dietary excesses by castrating him and hurling the genitals into the sea off Cyprus whence sprang Aphrodite (Roman Venus) the goddess of love. Visitors to Cyprus are taken in busloads to see the rock beside which this biologically improbable event took place. However, before inflicting this sordid fate on his wayward father Zeus did oblige him to disgorge all the children he had eaten, thus giving a sizeable population of gods to feature in the creations of Homer. It is not recorded whether the old man felt the benefit of this release of pressure on his digestive system which appears not to have been very efficient in the first place.

We were also just a short walk down a picturesque little path to the main road of Stalis. The town hardly existed at all until the advent of tourists, its origin resulting from the fact that it was the beach resort used by citizens of the mountain village of Mohos. The little path took us past a garden with vines that trailed over the wall to display bunches of grapes to which we occasionally helped ourselves with great restraint. You then join a road that runs by the fine beach only a few yards from the water of the bay. It was a particularly agreeable walk in a cool evening to go down there when other visitors or even residents were strolling and choose one of the outdoor restaurants where you could have good, unhurried service and an excellent souvlaki or meze in the balmy evening. Sometimes one of the restaurateurs would sit sharing some wine with us, ask us about where we came from and tell us about life on Crete. I had been intrigued for some time by the fact that most of Greece effectively shuts down in winter as far as the tourist trade is concerned. Obviously the weather is less good, but it is still likely to be much milder than in the UK. Giannis who owned perhaps our favourite restaurant explained to us that most of the families still either owned land or were related to those who did. They used the winter months to tend the olives and grapes which supported so much of the island`s economy. They really did not want to be distracted from this to look after foreign visitors. There was also the important consideration that, as we later became very aware, the Cretan calendar is packed with festivals when there is much feasting, dancing, eating and drinking. Tourists would be a major and unwelcome distraction from this important pursuit. Giannis confirmed what we suspected; that the Cretan economy had considerable independence from that of Greece as a whole. However, even with that he had little sympathy with the inevitable independence movement which had some support amongst romantics.

Suzie discovered that a moderate walk in the direction of Heraklion would take us to the Lychnostratis Folk Museum. It turned out to have been a splendid suggestion. This remarkable museum was set up in 1992 to house the impressive collection of artefacts gathered over many years by a writer and Professor of Opthalmology Yiorgogis Markakis. These items represented many aspects of Cretan life including clothing, furniture, agricultural implements, crockery and much more. The site is quite large and also contains a traditional farmer`s steading and a merchant`s house as well as an olive press and a distillery for the preparation of *tsikoudia* ,the local `raki` or liqueur. These were carefully constructed on the site during the 1990s, evidently using no modern machinery. You can therefore see many aspects of traditional Cretan life and even taste some of the food and delicacies in the café which is built to resemble the interior of a traditional Cretan home. The Dutch lady who was in charge at the time of our visit was delighted to share her love of the place and explain anything that was not obvious. We strolled round to an open area overlooking the sea where a young man was examining some stones with a well-thumbed textbook by his side. He looked up with a smile. Suzie had learned the Greek for "Good morning, how are you today?" and decided to try this out on the young man. His smile broadened. He complimented her on her Greek and asked if she could say anything else in the language. She turned to me for a translation of what he had asked which I provided. She thought for a moment and turned back to him proudly with the Greek for "I`d like a small cup of green tea please." She had learned this since this was her usual choice in any café we visited. The young man laughed and applauded her. He then explained that in fact she could have a cup of green tea, small or large, on the site in the café. I exchanged some more conversation in Greek and then we continued in English. He explained that he was an archaeologist attached to one of the universities, but one of his most pleasant duties was visiting this museum and helping to identify new finds. He was clearly very proud of his island and particularly pleased to meet people who were interested in more than the sun, the beach and the bars.

Our next trip was to Knossos itself. Like Pompeii in Italy it is very hard to convey just how impressive this site is. The story of its discovery is equally unbelievable. The very impressive Minoan civilisation came to an end around 1500 BC. Probably the major agent of its collapse was the huge explosion of the island of Thera (modern Santorini), perhaps the largest volcanic explosion in history. The weakened remnants that survived were unable to resist the incursion of the Myceneans who then occupied the city of Knossos for another two hundred years before dispersing. Nothing of the city was known until discoveries made in 1878 by one Minos Kalokairinos. It seems impossible now to believe the entire complex was buried under layers of earth which were being cultivated. Occasional finds, mostly of Roman coins with the word *Knossos* on one side and the image of a bull on the other might have raised a suspicion that there was more to be found but proper archaeological excavation did not begin until 1900 when the Englishman Sir Arthur Evans financed and supervised the project. It became a huge one. Evans was one of these remarkable Victorians whose life is designed to make all of us feel inferior. His father, John, had developed from being a helper in the stationery mill of his uncle to being a director of John Dickinson Stationery. John was an energetic man however who developed a serious interest in numismatics and archaeology. He maintained these interests, even becoming a Fellow of the Royal Society while also becoming very rich. Young Arthur, whose mother considered him intellectually feeble, often accompanied him on his search for artefacts and of course inherited much of the wealth. Some of his later tutors at Harrow and Oxford agreed with his mother`s estimate, but others saw in him a very original mind. The truth seems to have been that Arthur could not study what did not interest him. However, his interests were wide and he liked adventure. He spent time searching and excavating in Bosnia and Herzegovina, a dangerous area where you might well fall out with the Ottoman rulers or with the rival Austro-Hungarian Empire. Evans was highly sympathetic to the local people in their struggle against Ottoman rule, as Byron had been a little further south in Albania and Greece. He is in fact credited with having helped Yugoslavia to come into being as a nation. It appears that at various stages he was used by the UK government as a kind of unofficial ambassador. Evans had no concept when he began of how immense a project Knossos would be, but it put him on a par with the great German, Schliemann, who discovered the site of Troy.

We joined an excursion by coach to Knossos. Our guide was Claire, a young woman from Manchester who had only recently arrived and knew very little about Crete and less about the Greek language. That did not bother us but proved a source of irritation to Spiro, whom we met inside the gates of the archaeological complex. Spiro was to be our expert guide for the day. He was a man of medium height, perhaps forty five years of age. Whether he had dealt with Claire before or not we never learned but it soon became apparent that he held her in total contempt. He demonstrated this with breathtaking statements such as: "I explained all this to Claire but since she seems to understand her own language no better than Greek I`d better go over it again." Or, as we collected round his highly coloured umbrella (to enable dense foreigners to find him in a crowd) he would look wearily at Claire and say: "Claire, I have detailed all this twice already to you did none of it go in?" Claire showed remarkable good humour about this treatment which appeared to trouble her less than it did us. I was hoping to discover she had become expert in the ancient Greek martial art of *pankration* and might like to demonstrate it on Spiro. Gradually, however, we discovered that Spiro`s contempt extended beyond our luckless escort to embrace all of us also. It was tempting to ask him whether his wife had perhaps misunderstood his detailed breakfast instructions that morning or whether his bowel movements had been unsatisfactory. We concluded that he was probably a mental giant, or thought himself to be one, reduced by a philistine world to dealing with dull intellects. I have to admit that he did appear to know his subject well and poured out large amounts of information with his gaze fixed in the middle distance as if channelling it all from some ancient Minoan sage. Perhaps he was simply demonstrating how a noble mind could be overthrown by too many questions about how they cooked their chips in the ancient palace or whether evidence had been uncovered of ancient Cretan support for Manchester United. As with many other trips around ancient places you are likely to emerge from Knossos feeling that the history of mankind has not been uninterrupted progress.

Our next excursion contrasted in a number of ways with our day at Knossos. Here our guide was Elias, a large man who was a walking tribute to the fact that the island produced a lot of good food and wine, most of it apparently consumed by Elias. We soon realised that we had left the world-weariness of Spiro well behind us as our bus headed from Stalis into Heraklion. This was not to be our destination for the day, however. We were no longer in the antique world of Minoan Knossos. Elias loved Crete and everything about it. His mission appeared to be to make all visitors to the island wring their hands with bitter regret that they were not Cretan. In fact, his great pagan vitality was infectious. He reminded me of the equally exuberant if fictitious Cretan, Zorba the Greek, probably the best known book ever to come out of Crete, written by Nikos Kazantzakis, one of the island`s most celebrated authors. Elias did not actually dance as Zorba was frequently inclined to do, and for the stability of the bus that was perhaps as well, but you did feel his spirit was in a perpetual celebration of the landscape, the olives, the people, the wine, the seafood and the apparently endless number of festivals.

Elias proudly described Heraklion as we went through it and how much it had developed in recent years. He spoke about the war and how 12,000 German paratroopers had died taking the island. He described this event as if the invaders were doomed from the first, as if no amount of military power could ever succeed against the supreme vitality of Crete. The attack and occupation had been unspeakably awful, but there was something admirable and heroic about the way Elias described the island's recovery.

The coach then headed into the interior, through deep valleys between high peaks, visiting little villages which had barely changed in centuries and past vineyards and huge olive groves. Elias told us how special were the olives of Crete, as if all other olives had been mere experiments on the way to producing the perfection of the Cretan product. He told us that the preparation of the olives after harvesting and the production of olive oil had reached a standard probably unequalled in world history. The acidity of Cretan olive oil, he maintained, was only 0.3% whereas what we bought in supermarkets in Europe could well be 1.5% or worse. This was a persuasive argument which made us resolve only ever to consume Cretan olive oil until, back home, a little research made us realise that the acidity of olive oil was not a stable percentage. It would change over time. However, it does appear true that the Cretan product does begin with some advantage over most others. The acidity of the oil is a rather misleading term since it does not actually refer to the Ph content but rather to the presence of particular acids such as oleic acid. Elias became quite lyrical about the health benefits of olive oil, informing us that all skin conditions can be cured or alleviated by it owing to the presence of *squalene*. I had never heard of this substance and assumed Elias had simply invented it as a likely sounding, if little known, chemical. However, I believe it does exist and such research as has been done suggests he may be correct about its merits for the skin. He also explained that olive oil was very good for the heart and very helpful for those wishing to be slim. It was not immediately obvious how Elias could have known this. It appeared not to be the result of any experimentation on himself.

We eventually arrived at the village of Archanes, perhaps more a small town than a village. It`s a very attractive little place which has benefitted from European money. It has used it well, winning several awards as one of the best kept small towns in the continent. Elias told us that the archaeological museum contained some of the greatest treasures of the country`s remarkable history. This is not so strange since it is not far from Heraklion although our coach had taken a circuitous route to reach it. Oddly, we were not surprised when Elias also informed us that the wines of Archanes were probably the finest in all of Greece. The Kotsifali Cabernet, he advised us, was the equal of many of the great French vintages at much lower cost. I think we were becoming accustomed to our exuberant guide. Not that we thought him untruthful, but we did feel that turning down the volume on his mighty claims would probably get us nearer the reality. We were able to put this theory to the test quite soon. Before we left the coach to have a walk round Archanes Elias implored us to go to the square and visit the best patisserie in all of Greece and perhaps Europe itself. Not even the Champs-Elysées in Paris or the great bakeries in Rome could surpass it. We followed his directions and easily found the shop, a clean, spacious, inviting place with a range of tempting offers. We knew that lunch was almost due so we restrained ourselves a little. We bought some of the most inviting samples, ate them as we strolled past luxuriant bougainvillea, fruit trees and well tended floral displays and concluded that they were `quite good`.

We then strolled round to our assembly point in the centre of the village. From there we walked a short distance to a garden with long wooden tables in the shade of broad-leaved trees. They were set with cutlery and wine glasses. A slim, dark-haired smiling man in his forties welcomed us, shook hands with Elias and chatted to him. Meanwhile two waitresses invited us to sit. They then brought out jugs of iced water and large carafes of red and white wine. We sat with a German couple on one side and Danes on the other. The conversation began to flow immediately along with the water and the wine. Then the waiters and waitresses began the very Greek approach to meals, bringing out plates of houmous, tzatziki, taramasalata and stuffed vine leaves along with salad and baskets of pitta bread. No time is wasted asking people what they want. All of this appears and it is a style of communal eating which I find very appealing. Plates are passed round and people ask each other about particular items. You try something and have more if you like it or move on to another plate if you don`t. I assumed this was a pale imitation of the festivals Elias had so lovingly described. No doubt in a true Cretan community we would have had music from a couple of bouzouki players with maybe a Cretan lyre and a wind instrument such as an aulos or floughera. Then, satisfied with food and perhaps a little merry from the wine and, no doubt, raki, we`d all smash plates, dance and do a fair imitation of ancient pagans in the shade of the olive groves and lemon trees. Being the well-behaved northern Europeans which most of us were that was not going to happen, but we were thoroughly enjoying the company, the weather, the shade, the food and the festive atmosphere.

As the waiters brought out souvlakis, kebabs, cutlets, prawns and squid the bonhomie and camaraderie flowed like wine. As I ate, drank and chatted my mind went back to what we had seen at Knossos and in the Heraklion museum. Drinking vessels, plates, storage urns and serving dishes had all been found, moulded and decorated as important elements of their life. Some humbler tableware was in evidence too. I liked to think as

I sat in that shaded garden that we were enjoying an experience that had been common in the ancient life as well. Through all the turmoils of war, natural disaster and the vagaries of chance the simple enjoyment of good company, good food and wine triumphs and reasserts what is really important about life. The struggles of power, whether religious, political or commercial, are usually divisive and temporary. Events that bring us together and assert our common humanity are to be treasured. It is always tempting to think the Mediterranean people with their sunshine, stronger family and community life understand this better, but I`m afraid history shows they have been at least as inclined to invade and oppress each other`s countries as we bleak northerners.

Our final excursion on this visit was by coach going eastward. Even skirting the coast as we were doing we became fully aware of the massive mountain ranges that cross the island. The White Mountains, the Idi Range and the Dikti mountains have several peaks over 2,400 metres (8,000 feet). Amid them are deep valleys and plateaus, many of which are very suitable for agriculture. Our guide on this trip was Thora, a lady of around 35 years old. Her dark hair was severely tied back and she wore a shirt and navy shorts that would have been just as appropriate on a man. Her arms and legs suggested a woman who was no stranger to some demanding mountaineering. However, her lively eyes and attentive manner softened that appearance which might have seemed masculine but did not. Like Elias, she was very proud of her island and like him she was highly informative and interesting. Unlike him her comments and claims for Crete sounded very credible, even when surprising. She was well aware that thousands flocked to the Samaria Gorge, but told us about several others which were just as beautiful but less popular, giving perhaps a truer sense of the abundant natural world around us.

As we neared Elounda the coach stopped and our guide suggested we get out and admire the view. The road had climbed to a considerable height and when we got out we were greeted by the magnificent panorama of Mirabello Bay and on to the eastern tip of the island. Mirabello of course is an Italian word, paying tribute to the beautiful view, and is another contribution of the Venetian occupiers of old. At Elounda the coach stopped and Thora told us to be back in an hour. The next step on our day`s journey was to take a boat from near where the bus dropped us to the island of Spinalonga. Elounda is in fact a very ancient town, although the original settlement, known as Olous, was engulfed by encroaching sea. It can still be visited but only if you are prepared to dive into the waters of the bay. We knew very little about this place before the excursion and our impression was that it was attractive and well maintained. We noticed a very appealing café near to where the boats were moored and we decided to while away some of the time there. We went in and were immediately struck by how tastefully the place was furnished. It was not large and this probably added to the sense of comfort created by the well-upholstered seats in blue with red fringes and the very white woodwork. There was only one other customer there when we went in, a middle-aged man with silvery hair wearing what looked like an expensively tailored suit. The waiter behind the bar, a younger man, perhaps in late thirties, welcomed us and listened with a patient smile as we showed off our imperfect mastery of his language. The coffee was very good but we wondered a little how such an expensive looking café could survive in such a small town if this was an example of how busy it got. Only later did we discover that Elounda is one of the most exclusive resorts in Greece. The coves around it contained very expensive hotels and apartments, mostly in secluded spots for the very rich and famous to enjoy. It was likely that our café provided some expensive cocktails for glitterati. The mystery of its survival was solved.

The boat arrived on time and our group congregated to make the short sea journey to Spinalonga. This is an island or islet only about 170 yards from the pensinsula of Nissi which was itself made into an island by the Venetians who dug a channel across the narrow neck of land joining it to the mainland of Crete. The odd name almost certainly derives from a Venetian misunderstanding of the Greek *stin Olounda* meaning `at Olounda (or Elounda)`. When the Venetians occupied Crete in their quest to establish secure bases to resist the Ottoman Turks they built a number of fortresses on the island. In the case of Spinalonga the entire islet was used.

In 1903 a leper colony was established on Spinalonga. Leprosy, or Hansen`s disease, has of course always been regarded with terror and even superstition although only prolonged contact with it was likely to spread the affliction. Apparently more than 90% of any population is immune to it in any case, but this was not known at that time and, even knowing that, who would take the risk? Houses on the island had been abandoned by previous Muslim occupants so there was accommodation and a boat service could operate from the little town of Plaka on the main part of Crete to bring food and other items. The boat trip only took about 10 minutes. People of all types and ages came to the colony as sufferers and it is moving to hear how they used their different talents, education and experience to form a viable community despite the immense shadow that hung over them. It was by no means the only leper colony on Crete but it is the one that lasted longest. For much of the time the conditions endured by the colony were squalid. Greece suffered dreadfully from wars with Turkey and the First World War so resources were scarce and the needs of lepers were not foremost in Government minds. Everything began to improve in 1930 when a young lawyer Epameinondas Remoudakis arrived. Although afflicted with the disease himself, eventually losing a hand and going blind, he organised many improvements and was able to get valuable support from Athens. Eventually in 1948 a cure was discovered for the condition and the numbers in Spinalonga gradually reduced with the last twenty or so being taken for treatment to a hospital in Athens. I had hesitated a little before making the trip to Spinalonga but its situation is beautiful and the story, heart-rending thought it is in many ways, is also inspiring. The colony saw many examples of great courage along with compassion and a determination to value life as long as it lasted.

We had seen a lot in that first visit to the island of Crete but certainly left with the impression that you could spend a lot of time on it without exhausting its many attractions.

THE PINDOS MOUNTAINS

There is a land where wolves, otters, wild goats, wild boar and the brown bear roam freely amongst gigantic mountains and deep, lush gorges. The landscape is thick with varieties of trees and bushes up to the high peaks where even in summer there is snow. It has rivers of clear, pure water from which you can safely drink. There are villages where the houses of ordinary people are stone-built to a standard difficult to achieve elsewhere. There are small towns where the cafés and the *tavernas* serve generous quantities of pork, veal, chicken, wild or garden greens, very fresh salads and local wine. These eating places seem to have difficulty offering a bill that could possibly make economic sense for them. Yet, strangely it does. This is the world you find in the province of Epirus in North West Greece if you go into the mountains to Konitsa and the Zagoria villages. Sadly, it is also a world which has seen some of the most unspeakable horrors one set of people can inflict on another.

I had visited several Greek islands and some of the mainland. When I saw an opportunity to join a group spending most of a week in this little- known area I was glad to take it. The trip included some activities like gorge-walking and white-water rafting which are not part of my normal daily routine. However, if I wanted my usual lifestyle of exploring cafés and restaurants, art galleries and palaces then I was hardly going to appreciate the Pindos Mountains. I had to discover my inner frontiersman and laugh at awesome ravines and churning torrents.

We landed at Preveza airport in the early evening and were driven at disturbingly high speed in a couple of taxis for more than two hours to reach our first stop, the Konitsa Hotel. Fortunately our little group got on well from the outset and tacitly agreed that we could do without eating, drinking, toilet stops or breathing for two and a half hours. We were hurtling through some very fine scenery but hardly in an ideal way. It was clear to us that our destination was difficult to access and remote from our shrinking world where no peaks are too high or jungles too deep to be reached. Yet, inaccessible as it seemed in our modern age, this wild, craggy mountain world has been visited and settled for thousands of years by people with almost no technology whatever. The many caves in the region show it has been homeland to people from the Bronze Age and before. Historical records show they were followed by Acheans, Romans, Slavs, Vlachs and then the four hundred years of Ottoman Turks.

Even in our fatigued, hungry and oxygen- deprived condition we were impressed and delighted by what little we could see of the high mountains, tidy villages and vast perspectives in the setting sun. Our spirits rose still more when the cars stopped and we creaked and groaned out into the small hotel car park. Once our limbs were reassured a blood-supply was still possible we drifted in to a warm, friendly welcome in the old but splendidly modernised hotel.

On my first morning the view from my hotel window was one of life`s great experiences. I looked out on a wide panorama. Immediately below my window the town of Konitsa with its stone-built, red- topped houses spread out like lava down a steep hillside as it broadened towards the plain below and the E20 highway that leads to Ioannina. I could see vines and vegetable plots in the neat gardens below me, modern cars in the driveway and the remains of some of the grand mansions built by the wealthy during the Turkish occupation.

Beyond the town to the west on my left the river Aos wound away towards the huge mountains that mark the Albanian border, about 12 miles away. Mist was slowly rising from the snow-covered peaks. To the east was agricultural land as far as the eye could see up to more Albanian crags. I was aware of steep slopes on either side and later discovered that to the east was the giant Mount Smolikas, the country`s second highest mountain at 2637 metres (8651 feet) and to the south west was Mount Timfi at 2487 metres (8159 feet).Only Olympus in the east of mainland Greece at 2917 metres (9517 feet) towers over these giants. Later in the week we would get to know something of Mount Gramos further north at 2502 metres (8208 feet). To give this some context, the highest point in the British Isles is the summit of Ben Nevis in Scotland at 1344 metres (4,409 feet).

After breakfast our guides arrived. They were Nikos and Nikos. The smaller of the two had very dark-hair drawn back to a short pony tail and the olive skin common in the country. The other, who owns the outdoor activity company, Bee-Happy, had white hair but a young face with a ready smile. The dark-haired one, Nikos Ploumis, addressed us in good English in a resonant, clear voice which reinforced the first impression of a strong, vigorous man. We saw a lot of him during the next few days and, to a lesser extent of the other Nikos. We came to like both and respect the professionalism of both. Nikos told us something about the outdoor activities available and about the unique features of the area. Then we set off for our first day of activities.

Interesting history is often trapped in place names. Konitsa is not a Greek name. The most plausible explanation for it is that it is a Slavic word meaning `the place of the horse`. This seems likely since the modern

Polish word for `horse` is `kon` and `sta` resembles the word for a place or town in several European languages. Plaistow or Stow in the Wold show it in the UK. `Stadt` is the modern German word for a town and the word in Norwegian is `stad`. So, it seems likely that Slav peoples didn`t find the area inaccessible and the name seems to confirm the local belief that it was a centre for a horse market, which suggests many other potential buyers and sellers also reached it. Nor was it too far out of the way for the Ottoman empire, particularly when the notorious Ali Pasha came to power. Ali is described in Lord Byron`s long poem "Childe Harold`s Pilgrimage". He appeared to incur both the great poet`s admiration and his horrified loathing. Ali was not a Turk but an Albanian from the border town of Tepelene. In his youth he was a fearless, intelligent and ambitious brigand. Although the area was nominally under the rule of the `Supreme Porte `, the Turkish Ottoman empire, it was a lawless region with many local warlords. The Ottomans, taking a similar view to the western coalition in Afghanistan under President Bush and Prime Minister Blair, decided it was wiser to make use of this effective warlord than take on the expensive and alarming task of trying to suppress him. Ali became an admirer of the Ottoman janissary units and with their help he tamed his local countryside. He was rewarded with the task of overseeing the region of Rumelia as lieutenant. This area comprised modern Epirus and neighbouring parts of Albania and Greece. Ali seems to have been a good administrator and stimulated both trade and culture from his court in Ioannina, just south of Konitsa. For that reason he was regarded with respect and affection by many in this mountainous world who valued the stability in turbulent times. However, he was also guilty of hideous atrocities on a huge scale against both Greeks and foreigners. As with many powerful men he also appears to have had a monstrous sexual appetite. Evidently his harem of both males and females was huge, a fact that may have intrigued the sexually complicated Byron. Although Ali`s native language was the Tosk dialect of Albanian he normally spoke and decreed in Greek which was the tongue of most of his subjects. Greek is not much like Albanian which, although an Indo-European language, has little kinship with any other. Ali was also not especially loyal to his Turkish masters and gradually increased his own power, somewhat at their expense. It is thought by some that the independence he showed and his use of the Greek language gave inspiration to the nationalist movement that achieved independence from Turkey in 1831. Ali also makes a brief but memorable entry into French literature with an intriguing passage in the exciting and imaginative Dumas novel *The Count of Monte Cristo*. In it the Count, Edmond Dantes, plots revenge against the friends of his youth who had conspired to have him imprisoned. One is the fop, politician and socialite, Mondego, who married Dantes` childhood sweetheart, Mercedes. While a French officer in Greece Mondego is entrusted by Ali Pasha with the safekeeping of his wife and daughter, Haydée. The loathsome Mondego sells both into slavery. It is a very dramatic moment in the novel when Dantes arranges for Haydée`s release, brings her to Paris and enables her to take revenge on Mondego by testifying against him.

We drove down through the town. One of its claims to fame became immediately evident to us. This entire area including the Zagoria villages (of which more later) has been famous for some time for the quality of its stone building. Craftsmen in stone based in the Pindos Mountains have been in demand throughout Europe for many years. Even humble houses and shops look strong, well-designed and appealing.

Shortly after leaving the town we stopped beside the river Aos. Our walk was to begin by crossing the Konitsa bridge. This was constructed in 1870 by the builder Zeuga Frontso and is the largest unsupported stone bridge in the Balkans. We crossed it, the stone arch climbing quite steeply above the fast-flowing river before leading us to the other side. We then began along a broad path beside the water. On either side steep cliffs of limestone rock rose up to a great height. Rocky though they were, the slopes were covered with dense green bushes and trees.

Bright, vigorous-looking yellow, blue and lilac flowers sat in delightful bunches on the banks. The weather was warm and sunny, but comfortable for a walk. The river broadened and deepened as we went on, evidence that it was fed by many springs and streams which find their way through the porous calcite rock.

All of us noted the large number of caves in the high slopes on the far side. Evidently many had been used over the years by hermits. I find it striking that in such a beautiful and fertile country with, in my experience, attractive and friendly people, so many men (they are usually men) feel the need to turn their back on it. I suppose this just proves that the romantics did not invent world-weariness. H.V. Morton in one of his books about the Middle East notes how many believers in the early Christian era followed the odd example of Simeon Stylites by living on top of a pole. He points out that in a strong wind the traveller was in serious danger of lots of bearded, underfed men falling on him from a height. Simeon, incredibly, spent more than 37 years on top of pillars, gradually increasing their height until he was living fifty feet above the ground. This, of course, poses all sorts of questions about how he coped with the practicalities of life. Even his tolerance for complete boredom seems almost superhuman. Given pole-squatting as an option I think I would have found cave-dwelling almost attractive. Considering the circumstances during the reign of Ali

Pasha when being roasted alive was not an unusual reward for dissent the life-style seems almost sensible. As so often, I gave thanks for being born into a corrupt market economy with investigative journalism and foreign holidays. Even reality television seems a small price to pay.

At times this area seemed very reminiscent of Scotland where I live. The rugged scenery with greenery, high rocks and clear rivers is at times similar. However, geologically I think they are quite different. The hard rocks of Scotland are less fertile and also offer far fewer caves, not that there has ever been much demand for them in a land of sub-zero winters. Nor is Scotland quite so hospitable for the animal world. We no longer have the bears, wolves and bison that once roamed freely. Our most dangerous wildlife lurks in cities and emerges at important football matches.

As we walked we all got to know each other better. I spent some time talking to Nikos who was patient with my sometimes halting use of his language. Since his English was much better than his own estimate of it he understood some of the difficulties I had. Although Greek is an ancient Indo-European language, sharing kinship with most European tongues (the exceptions being the Finno-Ugric languages; Finnish, Estonian and Hungarian, brought in former times by Siberian tribes, and the inexplicably unrelated ones like Basque) it has some very peculiar features. Many of its words are very long and the construction of its tenses can lead the foreign speaker to deep despair. Perhaps this explains some of the world-weariness of the cave-dwellers. Nonetheless, almost 46,000 words in English come directly from Greek. Words like *psychic, tripod, arthritic, traumatic, profane, androgynous* and many others have simply been lifted from Greek, sometimes with changes of meaning.

We were all feeling quite triumphant in our first encounter with the outdoor, mountain world of Epirus when we came across a warning that things were about to change, although we did not recognise it as such. Sitting on a large rock by the tumbling waters of the Aos was a lean, old man. He had white hair and beard to match. His one garment was a long black robe or habit. His face was benign and he inclined his head in patient good-humoured greeting as we passed. Apart from his distinctive clothing he could well have been one of my elderly neighbours in Scotland waiting for a bus. One of our group asked me if I thought he`d appreciate a Polo mint, but we thought not. Thinking little of it we continued. Almost immediately, however, the gentle path began to slope ferociously upward. The merry conversation quietened and we quickly began to string out.

Up and up we went. A gasp was audible when Nikos pointed out the spire of the monastery to which we were heading. I had previously visited the spectacular, almost inaccessible monasteries of Meteora (actually not so inaccessible now since they built a road to them) so I knew that when Greek monks wanted to escape from the world they didn`t pussyfoot around. I was walking at the time with André (French name, English man) who asked me if Greek monks were known for their levitation abilities. "How the devil is the old chap on the rock going to get up this road otherwise?"He questioned. We kept our eyes open for hovering holy men as we rounded yet another bend to see yet another steep slope ahead. With each pace the tumbling Aos river below looked more distant and wild. A couple of our number decided that the old monk had the right idea and agreed that sitting on a rock was not a bad option. They had seen monasteries before. We pressed on and shortly encountered the answer to the transport problems of the monk. A young man appeared above us leading a patient-looking horse downhill. The Greek word for a horse is *alogo* which means `wordless`. It appears the Greeks have such respect for horses that they consider them fully the equal of a human but without the power of speech. Many people would feel equine behaviour easily surpasses that of humans in patience, forgiveness and helpfulness. It was intriguing to wonder what expletive we would have heard from the sturdy animal as he thought of the return journey with even a lightweight monk on his back.

The sun had come out and the temperature was now around 20 degrees. We were at an altitude of some 1600 metres and might have expected it to be cooler. We certainly did not want more sunshine. We were just resigning ourselves to the probability that each bend in the road would lead to another uphill with another bend when finally we saw the gates of the monastery and the small neat building about 50 metres beyond. Between the gate and the building was a yard bounded on either side by the sharp drop to the ravine below. Piles of cut stone stood in the yard, no doubt intended for renovations or, less likely, extensions to the building. We went through the brown iron door with its large rivets and found ourselves in a small courtyard with narrow porticoes on either side leading to further, smaller doors, no doubt leading to cells and a chapel. We did not intrude on that but crossed the courtyard to a series of perhaps ten steep steps leading up to a cross and a rail. Standing by the cross on the highest step the view down 1800 metres to the tumbling, writhing river was not for the light-headed. The sides of the gorge seemed to go down for miles with countless shades of greenery in the bushes and trees that pushed vigorously out of the creamy rock. Tiny birds darted here and there capturing invisible insects and if we looked upwards the steep sides of the mountains towered over us up to the now cloudless blue sky. Whatever the religious views any of us had I don`t think any of us felt that living in this remarkable place was the worst life-choice you could make, especially in the all-too- frequent turmoils that have struck this area.

We came back out of the monastery to see, first of all, some bright green lizards darting across the stones piled in the yard and the return of the horse with its aged but dignified passenger. He smiled at us in an indulgent way as if to say: "We`re not fools up here, you know." We could only agree. I spent a little time looking over the rail on one side down to a garden area where there were vines and a vegetable patch. Apparently there were only two monks at the retreat now, the elderly one we had seen and a young one. It was hard to believe they did all of the work in that garden, but perhaps they did.

Some of our group feared the return downhill more than they had the climb. It`s a question whether your lungs or your knees are the more troublesome. Nikos suggested a short detour down a path to the edge of the rock overlooking the river. Some of us followed him down a steep, winding track through the woods leading to a small clearing below which the river thundered past. We laughed in disbelief as we saw a fragile- looking bridge across the torrent. It consisted of rectangles of wood strung between two lines of rope. Overhead was another rope to enable anyone intrepid enough to use the bridge to steady himself. Outside of an Indiana Jones film I found it difficult to believe anyone would risk this crossing, but I know people do.

We continued down, following Nikos on other little detours that offered us different views and angles. Once we rejoined the main path we felt quite triumphant and I, for one, was hungry. As we strolled along I noticed movement on the steep rockface to our left. I looked up and saw a couple of wild goats leaping up the near-perpendicular cliff, clearly unaware of Newton`s invention of gravity. I was pleased to see this example of the wildlife of the area. The brown bears and wolves which we knew to be around somewhere were sensible enough to realise that human beings are far more dangerous than they are. I should like to have seen them, preferably at a safe distance on the far side of the river.

Lunch was now our priority. We asked Nikos to take us to Konitsa town where we would find something to eat. Without exploring very far we sat at the wooden tables outside a reasonable looking tavern. We were all too hungry to scour the place for fine cuisine. For some the main requirement was for any liquid they could be persuaded was beer. The taverna`s name was `Kapnismenos Tsoukali.` That odd name means `Smoking Pot`, in the sense of a cooking pot whose contents are smoking from heat rather than any more narcotic and decadent meaning. It is less strange when you realise that it is the title of a poetic work by Iannis Ritsos, one of the major Greek poets of the twentieth century. Ritsos came from a rich family in Monemvasia in the Laconia region of Greece so he was not a native of Epirus. However, his extraordinary life and the poems he produced strike a powerful chord in the hearts of many Greeks. He was still young when his family lost all of its wealth. His mother and brother died of tubercolosis when he was still a child and he too was later hospitalised with the illness. His father came down with severe mental trouble while Ritsos was still young as did his sister. His poetry was often overtly political, reflecting his communist sympathies. However, like his contemporaries Pablo Neruda in Chile or Hugh McDiarmaid in Scotland, many people find his left-wing poems less moving and memorable than his more intimate work where he brought a strikingly original expression of everyday experiences. Yet his political writings, which were very important to him, caused him to suffer imprisonment and exile on several occasions. Greece still has a strong communist movement, a fact fuelled by the outrageous corruption of many of their democratically elected politicians. It is no doubt understandable that the pious claims of Stalin sounded very attractive to a Greek generation robbed and savaged by the Nazis, torn by Civil War and then cheated by their own politicians. Perhaps it was kind that the full horror of Stalinism and its offspring were not too well known in Ritsos` life. However, at a time when it is very difficult for modern Greeks to know where to turn for a political salvation many still value the courageous honesty of Ritsos, even if the remarkable power of his intimate verse is lost on them. Perhaps Ritsos and others of his countryman would have preferred the order and stability even of a tyrant, a modern Ali Pasha, to the turmoil that has been too evident a part of their country`s history. Of course, Greece had the period of the Colonels between 1967 and 1974 who certainly provided tyranny but the colonels were blundering and incompetent, unlike Ali Pasha who mostly knew what he was doing.

We had not been seated long when Antonis, the proprietor, appeared. The pronunciation of his name in Greek corresponds to our word, Adonis. Margaret, sitting beside me, commented that this was not her idea of Adonis. Adonis, according to mythology, was a youth whose beauty caused violent jealousy between the goddesses Aphrodite and Persephone. The short, overweight gentleman with hair like a brush who came out to greet us seemed, at first sight, unlikely to cause much disturbance amongst goddesses. However, as he noted our uncertainty and offered to bring us out a variety of sausages, dips, salad, vegetables, chips and beer in the warm sunshine we loved the man. We sat, pleased with our first morning and with our wholly uninformed choice of Konitsa. It was a delicious moment when the pretty young waitress brought out beer followed by more beer and then sausages. There are times when *haute cuisine* which delivers a prawn with some rocket leaves and a spot of balsamic vinegar are not the best choice. We were much happier with the hot, tasty pork sausages, chicken pieces, salad, chips, wild spinach and courgettes which soon covered the table. As we paid our bill Antonis asked us how we intended to get back to the hotel which involved a demanding climb up a steep winding road. We all felt we had done enough of that for one day and told him we would take taxis. He surprised us by saying he and his waiter would drive us up in two cars. Of course we accepted this generous offer although if we had known how Antonis drove we might have hesitated. He handled his small car as he might have done a bus, veering alarmingly to the wrong side of the road to take the sharp bends before resuming his normal position of the middle of the road.

We all dined well and slept well at our excellent hotel. The following day we made the acquaintance of the other major river of the area, the Boidomatis. Our guides collected us again from the hotel and drove us to the Rafting centre where we were fitted out with rubber suits, helmets and life jackets. I looked at my companions who reminded me of a picture I once saw of a man fired out of a cannon. We all remained jovial. If any of us had seen the river we were to negotiate we might have fallen silent. We piled into the small bus that was now waiting for us and we were driven about four miles up the river to begin. Our guides with two younger employees of the company brought out the rafts, inflated rubber dinghies able to seat six at a pinch. They ensured they were fully inflated and then splashed water on them from the river. We assumed this was to cool them since a raft that seems fully inflated when warm may not be when cold water has surrounded it.

Nikos gave us instruction on how to sit in the raft and how to use the paddle. Then he told us the various commands he would use to enable us to deal with hazards. We were divided into two groups and set off. We noticed straight away that the Boidomatis is quite a fast-flowing river. However, it was a warm, sunny day and the countryside around us was beautiful. In our helmets, life-jackets and thick rubber suits we felt almost bullet-proof. We had little concern as we launched onto the apparently calm river. It wasn`t long before we met with the first turbulence. There may have been hearts in mouths but we followed the clearly shouted instructions and dealt with it. Shortly after that we realised we were hurtling towards a genuine danger. A tree had fallen across half of the river. It had fallen in such a way that it created a low bridge which might not allow is through. It was soon clear we would not be able to row around it so we all ducked as low as we could and realised why our helmets were essential. Clear of that we all smiled at each other in some kind of mixture of relief and triumph. However, there was not much time for self-congratulation. We were moving into genuine white water where the river looked deeper and certainly more turbulent. Nikos shouted instructions and we avoided the banks and a large rock protruding from the water. It was not long before we were in more churning waves, just as the river was heading for a sharp bend. Nikos` excellent English failed him and he shouted `back` when he meant `forward`. He soon realised his mistake but we were unable to avoid crashing into the rocky wall that rose up from the bank at the bend in the river. I think all of us, as we realised we could not avoid hitting the rock, wondered if this was going to be nasty and possibly painful. In fact we simply bounced off, paddled hard on instruction and were on our way again. The other boat was just ahead of us. They pulled in at a gravel beach and we joined them. We all got out of the boat and followed our guides into the woods and up some man-made steps carved out of the hillside. We soon found ourselves at a little, abandoned, partially ruined church. We went in and saw the walls and ceiling covered with the richly coloured icons of the Orthodox Church. Saints looked serenely down on us from the walls as we tried to imagine the world represented by this hidden little place of worship. Its ancient stones must have seen so much.

We were soon back in our dinghies and heading back into the current. We all took some time to admire the steep cliffs that rose sharply out of the water and which we would not have seen from any road or pathway. However, the restlessness of the Boidomatis soon called us back to our work and we paddled hard to navigate a couple of sharp bends. Then the river opened out and we saw ahead of us that we were approaching a weir. A weir is an artificial barrier that is placed across rivers, normally to help hydrologists measure the flow rate. They are not total barriers like dams. The river will continue to flow over the obstacle but in a different and more measurable pattern than in nature. They are, however, feared by canoers and Kayak users who often refer to them as `drowning machines.` Our confidence was reasonably high so we were not, at first, disturbed. This changed somewhat when we noticed that on the far left the fall of the river was not gentle. The weir had a different structure which meant the river suddenly dropped perhaps 15 feet or more in a churning, white- water cataract. We all felt grateful that we were heading for the broad, more gentle fall of the weir until we realised with horror that in fact the tumbling cataract was drawing us towards it and that no amount of paddling would keep us out. Our guide, Nikos, was sitting behind us, so we couldn`t see the expression on his face. Was it horror on realising disaster beckoned or serene confidence in the dinghies? We had no time to make a polite enquiry. At rapidly increasing speed we were sucked in to the swirling current and falling down into white arms reaching wildly up to draw us down. The boat became almost perpendicular and cold waves surged over us. There was nothing for us to do. We held our paddles upright as instructed, ensured we were well anchored with the one toe-hold and wondered how far into this maelstrom we would sink. White water engulfed us and for a brief time it was impossible to know if we were still on the surface or had plunged to the depths. The fact that we could still breathe, if we dared to, was, of course, a sign that it was not as bad as it probably looked. Very shortly after, we emerged, bouncing gently along away from what looked like a savage waterfall. Nikos shouted "Bravo". Soon we drifted calmly up to the rafting station where we had changed into the rubber suits, jackets and helmets for which we had been so grateful. We were a triumphant little group. The combination of exercise and relief had pumped us with endorphins and we felt like world-beaters.

The following day we were collected early. I was asked to sit in front with the white-haired, young faced Nikos. His English was less good so my imperfect Greek could be put to some practical use. We set off downhill to join the main road. We knew our destination was a dragon lake. Epirus has three of them. We were headed for the one high up on Timfi. We had little more information but since we had not been provided with weapons nor detailed instructions on combating dragons we assumed the danger was containable. The greater danger, evident from the outset, was in the dark, heavy clouds that covered the peaks of the Albanian mountains. We all had rainwear so we were prepared.

We turned off the main road and began to climb steeply. There were dense woods on either side and we began to see deep gorges beside the road. Soon we reached the first of the Zagoria villages. There are about 40 of these and they form an identifiable group in northern Greece. The name, Zagoria, is, again, a Slavic word which appears to mean "behind the mountain". It is tempting to link the name with other places in Greece with names like Zagora. That probably is misleading. The others probably are some form of the Greek *steen agora* which means `to the market`. The Zagoria villages all display the famed craftsmanship of their builders. The inhabitants are probably from a slightly different ethnic strain than others of the Greek population. There is a greater Vlach element to it, but the use of Slavic names suggests other origins are there also. There are also some of the Sarakatsani people whose language is a form of Greek with many words that are no longer found in the modern language.

This has led some to believe they are descendants of the original Greek people. In any event, the ethnic backgrounds of Greeks, Bulgarians, Vlachs, Macedonians and, no doubt, others, are thoroughly tangled. The language of the Vlachs has distinct Latin elements and one possibility is that they are descendants of Roman settlers. There is no such thing as a pure race in Europe anyway, and perhaps nowhere else. Having said that, it was some time before we came across any habitations at all. From the windows of the minibus we looked out on dense trees, deep gorges and high slopes. This was the home of brown bears, wolves, wild boar and wild goats. We saw none of them. What we did see at frequent intervals was very heavy rain. Fortunately the road was good for much of the way, but we eventually came upon a long stretch where major resurfacing was happening. Beside the road we saw workmen`s huts and heavy equipment parked beside piles of gravel. Mud on the road and the heavy rain made the driving difficult and unpleasant. We were all quite pleased when Nikos suggested we stop for coffee. He had telephoned ahead to ensure somewhere would be open in the next village, Skamneli. However, when we reached it the only café was shut. Our hearts sank a little since it seemed unlikely there would be anywhere else nearby in this magnificent but under populated mountain wilderness. However, we were wrong. A short drive took us to the appropriately named little settlement of Krisi, appropriate because that is the Greek word for gold and, on balance, I think we all would have been less impressed with the precious yellow metal than a good shot of caffeine.

We tumbled eagerly out, wondering what we could expect from such a remote and uninhabited area. We were now quite high up and on leaving the van we were not only hit by rain but by cold temperature too. We hurried into the small building. The first thing that struck us as we entered quite a large room was warmth. A stove in the middle of it was giving out impressive heat. The second thing was the look of stunned amazement on the face of some of the other customers. Most looked like workmen, probably from forestry or the road resurfacing, and continued with their drinks and chat. Several others viewed us with something like horror or disbelief. One thin, dark-haired young man with a three day growth on his chin struck me as ideal for the role of fugitive, terrified of discovery. Hollywood could have used him. He studied us as if he might hurl himself through the window beside him. His companion, an older, thick-set man, looked less thunderstruck but studied us more as if wondering how many of us he could flatten. The impression might have been still stronger if we had looked anything like athletic young spycatchers. Perhaps we stirred fears in that superstitious land of the walking dead. In fact it wasn`t long before they lost interest and returned to their

62

conversation. Whether that was about forestry matters or escaping a manhunt we would never know. It was much more likely that tourists and strangers were simply a very rare event in the Krisi café.

We had hardly sat down when the smiling proprietor appeared and took our orders. Then we were treated once more to a very Greek habit which I have not experienced elsewhere. Little plates of pastries, olives and cheese were brought although we had not ordered food. I have noticed this all over Greece. You can finish a meal, call for the bill and be ready to leave and they will bring pastries or fruit or cheese and olives and often a small glass of some heady local brew as well. Considering how little they normally charge that can`t make economic sense for them, but they survive. We tried various formulae in both Greek and English for pleading with them not to bring us any more food or drink but they always treated it as some kind of English humour that could not possibly be taken seriously.

After we left the village of `gold` we continued on upwards more and more steeply till finally we reached the awesomely anticipated `dragon lake`. Out we stepped to stillness. The rain had stopped but we were at altitude and it was cold. There was no wind and nothing seemed to be moving. Sharp, snowy crags rose up to a heavy sky as if hushed in expectation. No birds sang and there were no other humans around. How many people have visited a dragon lake? How many know what to expect there? Nikos pointed us towards the water. We glanced at each other and looked over. What we saw was most like a large muddy-looking pond. We felt that any serious dragon in it should be considering a house move. It was not Loch Ness. One of our group shouted "I see the dragon." We all looked up when another, a couple of metres away shouted "I see another one". No monster was climbing hideously from the swamp. No fire was being breathed. We all went over, peered in and saw tiny lizards darting around. `Dragon` was something of an overstatement. They are tritons, little creatures which would be no threat to anything larger than a water beetle. Nikos and Nikos smiled as their secret was revealed. Apparently there are three dragon lakes in the area and fire-breathing is not practiced in any of them. I have always been curious about dragons. They figure in most of the world`s mythologies. The Chinese mind often seems to be full of them as they organise their restaurants, landscapes and festivals. Germanic legend features them as retold by Wagner in *The Ring Cycle*. Hardly an English county or Scottish region is short of tales about them, with Somerset alone evidently thick with them at various times. A dragon allegedly protects Ljubljana and in Cambodia they have the Khmer dragon. In Welsh legend King Vortigern witnesses a battle between a green dragon and a red one. The Hungarian *sarkany* is a dragon. In Albania which, of course, just lies through the mountain passes from where we were there is the *bolla*, a giant, coiled, winged serpent which sleeps all year, only to wake, strangely, on St. George`s Day when, if he sees a human, he will devour him and fall asleep again. Native Americans have a `serene` dragon, a seven-headed one and both a Cheyenne and Iroquois lake dragon. Mexican literature has of course the wonderfully named *Quetzalcoatl*, the plumed serpent for whom the world`s largest pyramid at Cholula was built. In Scotland, as the world knows, we have the Loch Ness monster which attracts serious scientific interest. I once met a German limnologist on a holiday in Skye who told me he believed he could prove the existence of the monster by analysing the water. A limnologist is an expert on lakes. I had never heard the word before and at that time had no idea of its origin. However, the Greek for lake is *limni*. I don`t know whether he has ever had the chance to put his theory to the test, but if anyone had proved the monster was really there I`m sure we`d have heard. The interesting thing about dragons is that they have never existed. How could they have taken hold of the human imagination in such far-flung places?

We all climbed back into the van and Nikos drove us down the steep, winding road. It was now getting well into the afternoon. We were all hungry and none of us was quite sure what arrangement, if any, had been made for lunch. The weather continued to be gloomy and we were all rather quiet as the road downhill seemed longer than the uphill had ever been. Finally we came off the mountain and rejoined the main road. The mood was a little subdued, but far from downcast, since we had seen magnificent mountain landscape and, for most if not all of us, our first encounter with tritons. However, there was an audible gasp of anticipation when we reached the village of Kefalohori and turned into a pretty square with a well-maintained small garden in the centre. The name Kefalohori is Greek for `chief village`. I`m sure many of those reading this will know that it is the world capital of `mountain tea`. For those who may be ignorant of this phenomenon *tsai vouna* in Greek or `mountain tea` is a panacea known from ancient times. It is common in southern Europe and even in the Canary islands for its therapeutic properties. There are several varieties of it but they are all versions of the herb *sideritis* which is Greek for `iron man` or `the one with the iron`. It is probably a version of the plant known in English as ironwort. The origin of its name is not very clear since it doesn`t appear to contain much iron. It was however traditionally used to treat wounds suffered in battle which may have been inflicted by iron weapons. Equally likely is that the respect it gained in ancient times (and subsequently) for its properties made one as resilient as iron. It only grows at altitudes of more than 1,000 metres and can be grown domestically. The particular variety available in western Greece where we were is likely to be *sideritis purpurea* if taken from the wild. Considerable research has been done on the plant and appears to have confirmed that it contains anti-oxidants, anti-inflammatories and properties which help greatly with colds, influenza and breathing difficulties.

I have to confess that none of us knew, or indeed cared, about any of this. We were hungry and tea, however, nutritious, was not uppermost in our thoughts. We all went into what looked like an attractive little cottage. However, inside it was much larger. We were soon in a room with a long table in the middle set for ten of us. There were another three tables for four by the two windows looking onto the square. Men sat at each of them finishing some food although it was now very late for lunch. We were welcomed by a short, bespectacled, pleasant-looking blonde woman of around 45. Sitting in the far corner was a man perhaps a few years older with white hair and a well- tended moustache. We gathered that he was the husband and father since it was clearly a family business. He made no move to welcome us although he chatted amicably with Nikos who went over to speak to him. He simply sat in Olympian serenity watching everyone work and occasionally giving what we took to be well-directed instructions.

No time was wasted in establishing what we wanted other than our drinks order. The food had been decided before we arrived, although not by us. Almost immediately salad was placed on the table along with warm bread. This was followed immediately by bowls of tsatziki and taramasalata. Beer and soft drinks arrived and there was certainly no complaint about the speed of service.

I was sitting at the far end of the long table beside a young man placed at the head, or foot of it. He was perhaps 30 years old and had been one of the drivers in the other van. We had not met so I introduced myself to him and quickly realised he spoke no English at all. Since no one in the other car, apart from Nikos, spoke Greek, he had spent rather an unsociable day. I introduced myself and he turned out to be very chatty and friendly. His name was Kostas and he was a policeman in Konitsa. My naive view was that there wouldn`t be very much for a policeman to do in such an agreeable mountain retreat. I thought perhaps helping aging citizens across the road would be the extent of it although, fortunately, I did not express this view. One advantage of speaking a foreign language, especially a complicated one like Greek, is that your chances of blurting out thoughtless remarks is greatly reduced. For me, every remark in Greek takes thought. Kostas gave me an example of what he did. He told me that the previous week they had stopped a van from Albania on quiet roads. This had not been an accident or lucky chance. They had been watching this group. The van contained more than 20 kg of cocaine. The only regret was that the arrests they made were not of the big players. These were the footsoldiers, but nonetheless it was satisfying and could provide major information. He told me how much he enjoyed his work. A few weeks previously he had been part of a team that had gone to the coast to catch a group of divers who had swum from Albania with drugs. I asked Kostas if he thought narcotics should be legalised since this is currently an active debate on both sides of the Atlantic. It is argued that if the State provided drugs at a price considerably below that of the drug barons then the market would die for criminals. Addicts could be more open and treatment might be easier. Kostas had no sympathy with this view. His main reason was that he had a young son and he believed the job he did helped to protect the boy. I didn`t know enough about it to argue. Anyway, Kostas seemed to enjoy catching the smugglers so perhaps there wouldn`t be much to do if the law was changed. Very possibly they would just smuggle cigarettes, alcohol or people instead.

Quite soon pork kebabs appeared followed by lamb steaks and sides of mutton. Kostas told me that all of this was local. I asked if much fish was eaten in the area since I knew some was caught in the rivers, but apparently not.

They liked their meat. It was certainly very tasty and succulent.

At the end of the meal Margaret, one of our number, called me over. She had been enjoying some of the mountain tea and she asked me to enquire of our hostess whether she grew it in her garden or gathered it wild. Our hostess animatedly confirmed that it was wild and she regularly went to the mountains to get the best leaves. The implication was that the garden version was an inferior product. By this time we had all eaten well and were content. Our only problem was how we would deal with the hotel dinner that would be served in not much more than an hour.

On our final day in Konitsa the minibus took us to some of the other Zagoria villages, particularly to Aristi and then on to Vikos. Here the spectacular Vikos gorge begins. The gorge is around 32 kilometres (20 miles) long and at times is 915 metres (3,000 feet) deep. It is often said to be the finest walk in Greece. There are two main paths down to it. The one beginning at Monodendri is the more challenging but is badly maintained and thought to be dangerous. The one from Vikos is a shorter descent and in good condition. Vikos itself is small but it has two tavernas facing each other across the square. We parked beside one and began along a level country path. This quickly took us to a viewpoint from which we could look far down at the river Boidomatis tumbling over large boulders on its journey through the gorge. As we turned from that an elderly but strong looking man approached us carrying a long-handled scythe. I wondered for a moment whether *Chronos* the ancient Greek god of time had risen from the depths of the Boidomatis to have a word with us. *Chronos* is not to be confused with the titan *Cronus* although he often is even in mythology. Both carry a sickle since time of course harvests its own children at the end of their life-span. This gives us the more modern image of Father Time with his cloak and sickle. Since I imagined an ancient god would be happier with Greek I addressed him and asked if he was local. He answered me in good English. I might have explained to him that if I had needed practise in my own language I could have stayed at home, but I thought that discourteous and I didn`t know how much provocation Father Time needed before he started harvesting people. It turned out he was a retired teacher who now reared medicinal herbs, following the ancient tradition of the travelling Vikos doctors who were, we gathered, quite renowned. Since we were still feeling quite sprightly and most of our group saw therapy as a litre of beer or the local red wine he did poor trade with us. He did, however, stay long enough to tell us that *vikos* is a Slavic word for echo since this can be experienced at various places in the gorge.

The smaller Nikos led us to the beginning of the descent. He suggested it would take us about one hour to go down and a little more to come up. When we looked down at the tiny church that represented our destination a number of us wondered whether we were really ready for this. Three of our group decided they would be happier getting to know the tavernas and the rest of us set off. There was a well-made path of stones all the way, sometimes in the form of steps. The stones were, however, quite smooth and could be treacherous. Those whose knees were still aching from our first walk took their time. The scene was magnificent with varieties of green trees and bushes all the way down. There were bunches of colour on either side of the gorge from lilacs, crocuses, gentians, grass-of- Parnassus and many varieties of orchid. Ominous-looking birds of prey hovered and circled above us. I wondered if they were fond of the tourist trade for ghastly reasons but Nikos explained they were Egyptian vultures that enjoyed the thermals from the gorge and found they could hover readily as they searched for any of the abundant wildlife they ate. There were lizards, various types of rodents, snakes and tortoises. I don`t think they preyed on tortoises, but I did recall for a moment the alleged death of Aeschylus, the first of the great ancient Greek tragedians. The story goes that a particular type of eagle in Greece does prey on tortoises. To crack their hard shells they carry their quarry upside down in the air until they spot a boulder on which they can drop the doomed creature. One eagle in his haste to have lunch apparently thought he saw a promising boulder which was, unfortunately, the shiny bald head of the great tragedian. Aeschylus then, famous for great works in his lifetime, is, I believe, the only recorded example of death by falling tortoise.

MY SECOND VISIT TO RHODES

Rhodes is the third largest of the Greek islands and is said to be the one with the most hours of sunshine. I had visited it some years before when I had stayed in a hotel in Ialysos, near the island`s capital, Rhodes town.  I had made that first trip with the Solo`s company with which I have often journeyed abroad. Its format means you travel with a group of people who don`t normally know one another. You stay in the same hotel and have the opportunity to have meals and excursions together or explore on your own. The Solo`s company organises excellent excursions also which cater for a range of needs and interests whether your taste is late-night dancing, sea trips or local history. My second trip six years later was with a different company with the same concept but carried out with far less efficiency and local knowledge.

There are many reasons for visiting the island of Rhodes. The weather is the main attraction for many people. Its proximity to the Turkish coast means it can be combined with trips into Anatolia. It is a green island with some fine scenery. The people, as in most of Greece, are charming and friendly and the options for accommodation are, nowadays, wide-ranging. Personally, all of these aspects appeal but I am of course also interested in the language and culture of modern Greece. In addition, the history of

Rhodes is of particular fascination. The modern administration takes great care to nurture this aspect.

The island has been occupied since the Neolithic age and traded from the earliest times with Phoenicians, Egyptians and the various inhabitants of the other Greek lands, whether Achaeans, Minoans, Myceneans (possibly the same people as the Achaeans) or Dorians. There are perhaps two episodes in its history of particular interest to the modern world. One is the strange tale of The Colossus of Rhodes. The other is the island's connection with the Knights of St. John, the so-called Knights Hospitaller. Of the first there is no remaining sign in the modern island. Of the second there is an impressive amount. The large complex of residences and palaces created by the Knights can be visited by the Venetian harbour in Rhodes Town where you can walk through the old area into the modern city and back.

For my second visit I was booked into a hotel in Lindos. This very pretty little town by the sea has figured strongly in the history of the island from the earliest times. I had joined a boat trip to it on my first stay on the island and had walked up the 166 metres of the steep, winding path from the harbour to the ancient, ruined Acropolis round which the town grew. It is set about 55 kms south of the capital on the east side. I flew from Glasgow. My flight was delayed by an air-traffic-controllers strike in France and I arrived at the hotel after eleven at night. The company's rep, Emma, was there to meet me and took me to the `overflow` hotel across the dusty country road where a room had been reserved for me. Each of the rooms was accessed from an open passageway that ran along the outside on three levels. To obtain my room key we went to one of the rooms and hammered on the door. This was when it first occurred to me that my hotel may fall short of the highest standards of accommodation. After some time the door was opened by an unhappy-looking man of middle age wearing shorts and a red vest. This was Antonis, the manager. The news that a hotel guest had arrived and wanted access to his room was not well received by him. He picked up a key and shot off along the passage. Emma wished me `goodnight` and as I picked up my bags and turned I saw the red vest disappear round the corner. When I reached the corner I heard footsteps on the stair and assumed this was the bearer of my room key. Despite my having two heavy cases, being perhaps fifteen years older than the speeding Antonis and unaccustomed to the considerable heat I attempted to catch up. I reached the first landing and there was no sign or sound of anyone. After a moment I heard a voice. I looked around and saw Antonis at the far corner on the passage below me. It was, I assumed, the first time he had looked round since darting off with the key. We had clearly wakened him from a pleasant sleep. I confess that I also dislike being wakened from sleep but I could hardly be blamed for their failing to make some sensible arrangement for the possibility of a late arrival. It is, after all, not an unheard of phenomenon in the annals of the catering industry. I lumbered back down, noting that this `hotel` had neither late arrival facilities, night porter facilities nor even `welcome with a nice smile after your long flight` facilities. I took the key and restrained my urge to thank Antonis and wish him goodnight. I also restrained less friendly urges.

The room itself was clean but no better than basic. At first I wondered if the disgruntled Antonis had ushered me into the hotel oven considering the extreme heat. The bed and toilet facilities persuaded me otherwise. The temperature had the unexpected benefit of apparently sapping local mosquitoes of their usual bloodsucking vocation. I undressed and lay on the bed, idly wondering if air-conditioning had yet reached Lindos.

The following day I walked the short distance past a few fields of goats. Even at nine in the morning the temperature had been oppressive. By eleven it was already above thirty degrees and was to get hotter. In the fields the goats were grazing although with the naked eye nothing edible appeared to be available on the ground. I passed a supermarket which served residents of my hotel and its two neighbours. I then reached the main road which was the one that led up to the capital, Rhodes town. Another couple of shops and a small restaurant clustered there and across the road was a sizeable bus park where the various coaches that took trippers around the island congregated each day. A road went downhill from there to a square where taxis waited. A few steps farther led into the town itself with shops and cafés on either side of the avenues. Although broad enough for a few people to pass each other they were more passages than roads. The occasional car or van would creep with infinite patience along them. Almost immediately you reached the donkey enclosure where people gathered to pay for a ride on the durable little creatures up the hill to the Acropolis. The handlers varied in age and were already eagerly under way with their work. This would be early in their most profitable season and there was money to be made. I didn`t envy them much more than I did the donkeys since they too had to walk up the steep hill with every rider. Some were no longer young but none was fat.

The passages in Lindos twist and turn and often afford views of the lovely bay below. The shops are all bright and most of the proprietors were smiling hopefully. I decided it would be prudent to buy a hat. I rarely wear hats in Scotland other than the woolly ones I use in winter to protect head and ears from the cold. I had bought a broad-brimmed one in Australia a few years before but had neglected to pack it. The increasing ultra-violet bombardment suggested this was a priority. How can the thing be 93,000,000 miles away and still so hot? Whatever the answer to that (and I'm perfectly sure there is one that I would fail to understand) I was certainly in the right place. Hats sat in large piles around me in the shops. However, I wanted one with a little style and they were not so plentiful. I found one that appeared to be straw but was actually some kind of plastic moulded in China. It was modestly priced so I took it. The cheerful lady who served me seemed delighted that I could speak Greek. It gave her licence to express her lament that the wares she sold had to be imported from so far away. When she was young, she reminisced, her father and her uncle would both make hats which she thought greatly superior to what she was selling. She thought the Chinese probably had machines which could turn out a thousand hats a minute whereas her father might take a month to finish one. That was the difference. I remarked that progress and improvement are not always the same thing. She greeted this observation as worthy of the great philosophers of her magnificent Hellenic culture. I left the shop feeling I had given her a gem to ponder on. I put on my mass-produced Chinese hat and appreciated the broad brim. I then felt protected from the increasing ultra-violet rays. Thus armed against the ancient sun god Helios I decided to look for a decent café. In fact that is not difficult in Lindos. I went into the first one I passed which was only a few steps from the hat shop. It was an open doorway with white tiled stairs leading upward. I saw neither customers nor staff at this point. I reached the landing and a young waitress smiled at me. She told me I could go further up since the view was worth it. I obeyed and decided I had been well-advised. I found myself as the only customer in an area large enough for twenty tables. This was the first of several such roof-top establishments I enjoyed during this week. Bougainvillea with large lilac flowers trailed along the walls and I was high enough to look over the rooftops to the bay, a natural inlet like a circle of which two thirds is land. It was obvious why a settlement would have arisen around such a favourable shelter from the open sea. It is large enough to hold a large number of vessels and the hill that rises steeply from it to the Acropolis would provide a wonderful lookout to spot approaching enemies.

The sun was relentless but the parasols at the table provided shade. Sitting there with the sunlit view of the steep hills that surrounded the town down to the very blue water was a genuine pleasure, a very Hellenic experience. The young waitress came up and I practiced my Greek, learning that she was from Athens. She was working here to make some money before beginning studies at university. As usual I took the opportunity to get a little instruction from her. Learning a language is an endless task. Even in your native speech there are words and expressions you don`t know or don`t use correctly. In a foreign tongue that is inevitable. I have never found a Greek who thought it a burden or a nuisance to help me with their language. They are proud of it and proud that I should want to speak it.

I looked over to the high hill above the bay where I could see lines of visitors on the path to the Acropolis. More were descending than going up. Hardly surprising since the steep climb would be much easier before the sun was fully up. The Acropolis was probably first built in the eighth century BC to honour the goddess Athena. One myth suggests Danaos, legendary founder of the Greek race, stopped here on his way from Egypt to mainland Greece and founded the temple. It is certainly true that there were extensive interchanges between Egypt and the southern Greek islands in pre-Christian times. Indeed, she may be a version of the Egyptian goddess Neithe. She is one of the most important of the female deities who were so prized in the eastern Mediterranean in antiquity. Her domain was a wide one encompassing knowledge, purity, crafts, knowledge and wisdom. I find it difficult to avoid the view that this reflects a much more balanced attitude to the sexes than is evident in the later Middle Eastern religions. These have all too often led to appalling treatment of women in favour of extremely bloodthirsty patriarchs. I often think of the words of the Irish poet, Yeats:

"Odour of blood when Christ was slain

Makes all Platonic tolerance vain

And vain all Doric discipline."

The temple has been destroyed and restored several times down the ages. It is currently a ruin, but its attraction remains strong even in the searing heat from which I was sheltering. Athena was, interestingly, always regarded as a virgin, *Athena Parthenos,* which explains why the magnificent temple to her in the city which bears her name, Athens, is called The Parthenon. No doubt early Christianity also found it easier to recruit pagans by assuring them they could go on worshipping the virgin deity, simply with a change of name.

I was joined in my rooftop, sun-drenched solitude by a German couple laden with maps and books along with at least three cameras and two mobile phones. We got talking and I discovered that, first of all, their extensive cargo of equipment did not include a bottle of water. The waitress was in the process of putting that right. I then gathered it was their first trip to Greece. They were intrigued that I had visited so much of the country and asked me which places I would recommend. I suggested they try all of it since I hadn`t been disappointed by any of the islands I had seen nor by the mainland. I felt this was not the answer they had been hoping for. Perhaps they felt this indicated a vulgar lack of discrimination in me but they asked me to explain more of what I had seen and liked. They began noting my comments with furious and slightly embarrassing zeal. I felt like a schoolmaster. This was only surpassed by the desperation with which they guzzled a bottle of water each and asked for more. I was amazed they had been able to summon up any interest in my views on Crete and Athens and the Dodecanese when apparently so dehydrated. Noting my enthusiasm for visiting Greek islands they asked how many I thought I would be able to get to in my lifetime. I felt perhaps another 25 might be possible. They clearly wondered how I would reconcile myself to the inevitable frustration of not seeing more. I suggested I was hoping Pythagoras had been right in his theory of `metempsychosis`, better known as reincarnation. They nodded as one might do to humour a stranger who suddenly announces he is really Napoleon or has recently been abducted by aliens. They treated my remark with more gravity than I had intended.

Partly motivated by the extreme heat, I had booked passage on a cruise to the little island of Symi, about two hours across the sea from Rhodes. I had done this trip before and had liked the island a lot. As before, the excursion would give us time in the colourful main town, Gialos, in the sheltered harbour of the Nimborios gulf, before taking us round to Pantoleimon, the splendid monastery of St. Michael. The name. Pantoleimon, means `the all-merciful`and, as I have noted elsewhere, there are many stories of miracles attributed to the mercy of St. Michael. This is, of course, not a rare phenomenon in Greece or indeed other parts of the Mediterranean. The best-known `miraculous` site is probably the church of the virgin on the island of Tinos to which remarkable achievements are attributed.

Symi itself, although small, used to be very prosperous as a result of both sponge-diving and shipbuilding. These were encouraged and sponsored under Ottoman rule. Turkey is, after all, only around 6 miles from the little island. By the beginning of the 20th century it allegedly was producing 500 ships a year, a remarkable figure. However, the rise of steamships was fatal for this industry and its reputation for sponge-diving was eclipsed by that of Kalymnos. These industries have gone, but the fine buildings constructed as a result of the consequent prosperity still form much of the charm of Gialos. Now tourism, overwhelming at times, provides the income.

Since the boat would depart from the harbour at Rhodes town a coach was to collect passengers from various pick-up points around the island. I had an early breakfast and then strolled back past the goats eating their invisible food to the main road where the buses stopped. A number of people were standing in different groups. Some were awaiting the service bus which stopped at various locations up to the capital. Others were, like me, there to be collected by one of the excursion coaches. When I arrived at this gathering point most of the people were dressed in shorts and tee shirts or other casual wear. I noticed a lady of around 55 who was rather more elegantly dressed in a long, lilac skirt and a yellow top. She also had a white, broad-brimmed hat with a blue ribbon which had obviously cost her rather more than my own piece of Chinese plastic. It was lying beside her on the bench where she was sitting. I noted as I approached that she looked a little anxious. She hurriedly removed the hat from the bench, assuming I might want to sit there. I smiled and held up my hand to indicate there was no need for her to make space. I was happy to stand since I'd be sitting for a while on the bus and then the boat.

A number of coaches pulled up and all of us went up to them to establish which excursion they were serving. The elegant lady looked a little more anxious with each one that turned out not to be ours. We were the only two left at the pick-up point when one arrived with SYMI clearly advertised on the front window. I gestured to her to climb on board first and with an anxious glance she did so. I followed and sat downstairs. At first she sat across the aisle from me to my left. However, almost immediately she moved and went upstairs. I thought no more about it. After a pleasant half hour we arrived at the harbour where several large ferries waited. Symi was by no means the only destination for these ships. Some went to Kos or Piraeus, the port of Athens. Others went to Karpathos or Crete and some to Marmaris in Turkey. Lots of buses had pulled up and lots of people emerged with lots of guides trying to organise them. I waited beside Peter, our escort for the trip, until he led us off. As I stood there the elegant lady stepped down from the bus and came directly up to me, still looking anxious.

"Excuse me," she began. "Will you help me? I don`t know where we have to go and I`m scared."

Her English was good but she was obviously not a native speaker. I smiled and replied.

"Don`t be scared. We`ll just be following our escort onto the ferry. Stay with me and you`ll be fine. It will be a nice crossing."

She relaxed a little and thanked me.

"Where are you from?" I asked, unable to place the accent.

"I`m from Russia. I live in Samara on the Volga."

"You`ve come a long way."

She felt able to smile a little now.

"Everywhere is a long way for me, but I love to travel."

Peter signalled to us and we began to move. He had told us which ferry we were heading for anyway and he also explained in detail what time we would arrive, how much time we would have there and when to reconvene. I was not certain that I wanted to have the lady`s company for the whole day and was not sure whether she wanted mine once she understood the plan for the trip. I think I am a reasonably friendly person, but there are people whose company would ruin my day. Someone who talked incessantly, especially without establishing whether I had the faintest interest in their conversation, would come into that category. So would those (often the same people) who feel the need to enlighten me about salvation, the limitations of American foreign policy, Israel-Palestine or their unsatisfactory son-in-law. I had no way of knowing whether this lady would come into any of these categories. The fact that she travelled alone could be seen in either of two ways. She could be someone who was sustained by the experiences of travel without the need of constant company. That would be good. On the other hand, she could be such an unbearable person that no one would travel with her. That would be bad. My initial impression tended more to the first possibility. In any event, I would want to find a tactful way of disengaging myself if that became necessary. I had, after all, already suggested she stay with me although I had not really meant for the whole day.

We boarded as the heat from the sun was increasing and it was pleasant to sit on the deck with something of a breeze. I learned that my companion was called Larissa. She was married with children and grandchildren, but her husband was a beekeeper who could not get away in summer. He didn`t much like travel in any case. She was an English teacher which explained her fluency in the language.

We arrived at Gialos on Symi in the late morning. I decided to offer Larissa the possibility of continuing without me. I explained that I was a caffeine addict who intended to find a good café overlooking the very picturesque harbour before exploring. She was welcome to join me for coffee, but now that we had arrived she might wish to see as much as possible of the little town. The inlet from the sea is V-shaped and shops and restaurants cluster along the arms of the V. The hillside rises on either side with neoclassical mansions in various bright colours overlooking the bay. These dated from the prosperous years of sponge-diving and boat-building, but tourism was offering them a new lease of life. I had visited the town before so felt less urgency, although I did like the idea of climbing to the castle of the knights of St. John at Horio a few hundred metres above the town. Larissa said she didn`t want coffee but would like to join me again after she had looked at some shops and I`d had my fix for the morning. She was not deterred by the prospect of the ascent.

I chose a small café called The Opera House and sat looking at the blue sea, the various boats in the harbour and the green hillside rising with its mansions across the water. A tall, erect, elderly man came up for my order. He had a self-possessed air about him and I took him to be the owner. He nodded to my request and soon brought me my coffee and a croissant which I had not ordered but which looked quite appealing. As I sat enjoying my refreshment a small, battered truck rumbled past. Sitting in the back were five or six men wearing Arab headgear.

"Refugees," said the owner from his seat, a little to my left.

"From Syria?" I asked. He nodded.

"That must be a problem," I suggested.

"A big problem. A very big one."

I finished my coffee, thanked the gentleman who nodded graciously and turned towards the town. I saw Larissa straight away looking at some of the shops just a little way down. I took it that she wanted to have more of my company. We walked on into the lively, colourful little town and came to a small bridge over an inlet from the sea. She asked me if I would take a photograph of her and handed me an elaborate-looking piece of apparatus more like an expensive coffee-maker than a camera. I was just taking up a suitable position when a small, dark-haired lady aged perhaps forty asked if we would like her to take our photograph, assuming we were a couple. I decided that would do no harm although I soon sensed a hesitation in Larissa. After the picture was taken I asked the lady where she was from since I was sure, despite her colouring, that she was not Greek. She told us she was from Israel. Greece, to its credit, has managed to maintain good relations with both Israel and the Arab world and increasing numbers of Israelis holiday in Greece. It is not too far to travel and the climate is, I believe similar. I was not surprised when she moved on that Larissa asked if I would take another just of her. I agreed, recognising that I was, understandably, to be deleted.

Larissa bravely enthused about joining me in the climb up to Horio and we quickly found the steps leading sharply uphill. It was a hot day and we had no idea how many steps we would have to climb. We passed some fine houses which were in need of serious repair, probably a sign of the hard times from which tourism was rescuing the place. The views over the bay became increasingly impressive but both of us were feeling the effort. A couple, perhaps in their late forties were just coming down.

"It doesn`t get any easier," said the man, merrily, noting our red faces. I asked if we were near the top. He thought for a moment and advised that we were probably almost half way. He did however advise us that a local housewife was sitting a little way up selling a cup of water and a sprig of lavender. "That doesn`t happen in Halifax," he advised.

In view of that information and the need to fit in lunch before leaving Symi we decided to take some photographs from the height we had reached and go back down. There we went into some of the traditional restaurants which had fresh fish on offer. This was not an enterprise Larissa had tried before and she was a little uneasy at first about inspecting and leaving. At the fourth or fifth one, a little back from the main street, we were welcomed by a thick-set man with a couple of scars on his face. Had he been a brigand, smuggler or freedom-fighter who had led a life of adventure and intrigue? A friend who knew the island later advised me it was more likely he had been a sponge diver in his youth. Apparently that occupation was about as dangerous as you could get. In any event he had a welcoming manner and we thought the setting cool and colourful. The fish looked as good as any we had seen and we decided to share a large red bream.

After what proved to be an excellent lunch we returned to the boat which took us round to Pantoleimon and the monastery of St. Michael. Since I had seen it before I left Larissa in it after I had taken a cursory look and told her to find me later in the considerably upgraded café just beside the main entrance. I had been pleased to have Larissa`s company but I wanted to write some notes and read some of a Greek newspaper I had picked up. I was absorbed in that for a time. When I looked up I noticed the Israeli lady who had earlier taken our photograph was seated at a nearby table. We exchanged a smile.

"They`ve upgraded the place and the coffee since my last visit," I observed.

"Are you a connoisseur of coffee?" she asked.

"Hardly, but I like to be able to distinguish it from engine oil which is sometimes difficult."

"Do you know where you get the best coffee in the world?" she asked, clearly about to tell me."

"I can think of a few candidates but I`d have to say the place where I`ve had the most consistently good product is Melbourne, Australia. Where would you recommend?"

"The best coffee in the world is in Jerusalem," she said with enough of a smile to reassure me her survey of candidates was not comprehensive.

"I`ve never been there," I confessed. "Is Jerusalem as hot as it is here?"

"At least five degrees hotter."

"I may settle for inferior coffee."

After that full day`s excursion I decided to haunt Lindos for the following day. I was adapting to the heat although I set off from my room, still hot enough to scramble eggs, so that I could reach the shaded passages of Lindos before the sun was fully up. I walked along past the fields of goats, still apparently digesting fresh air, reached the main road with its two or three shops beside the bus stance where I had waited for the coach to Symi. I crossed, went through the car park, down a short flight of steps and walked along the downhill road which led to the town and, ultimately, to the beach. The road had no pavement and the stream of cars going down and up seemed endless. At the bottom of the road was an open area or square, the Plateia Eleftherias. A large, old tree rises up from the centre of the square and there are steps around it where you can sit and watch the traffic stewards, patiently and good-naturedly herding the stream of cars round the tree and down the road to the beach. Delivery men also arrive and park their vans haphazardly as they carry water, beer, fruit or whatever else into the shops in the shaded passages. I expected yells of annoyance from drivers blocked in by these vans or taxi-drivers having to make awkward manoeuvres round them, but everyone appeared content that this is simply the way a Greek town functions.

I sat in Plateias Eleftherias for longer than I had intended. There was shade from the tree, but that was not the only reason. The bustle of the little town was endlessly entertaining. I thought of the great travel writer, H.V. Morton, who visited Rhodes in the early nineteen thirties, researching his book *In the Steps of St. Paul*. He refers to Lindos as "a quiet, lovely place, full of butterflies, bees and curiously silent brown children." That was certainly not how I would describe the scene around me as I sat in the shade of the old tree. The only insect life I recall is the flies around the donkeys whilst the children seemed neither more silent nor more brown than those I had come across in other parts of Greece. The only point where we are in agreement is that Lindos is lovely. Some people will feel progress has destroyed the silent charm of the place, but it should perhaps be remembered that in the fourth century B.C. this was probably the busiest part of Rhodes. Lindos was a centre of power. It was not always a tranquil backwater before modern tourism.How the butterflies and bees felt about that I cannot say.

Adaptability is the key to survival in most walks of life. It obviously applies as much to towns as to plants and animals.

Eventually I decided to abandon my seat beneath the tree in the Piccadilly of Lindos. Of course I like to find a suitable place for my morning coffee, but I had other motivations. On my way down the steep road I had noticed a café with a particularly striking setting. It was on the edge of the hill that tumbled sharply down to the bay perhaps 80 metres below. I walked back up the 20 metres or so to its entrance. One or two locals, as I took them, sat on the narrow terrace beside the busy road, smoking and debating. I thought this odd and wandered through to the sizeable lounge at the back which was deserted. I greeted the young, bored-looking waiter and asked if he minded if I sat at the far end where the series of large windows gave a panorama of the bay across to the Acropolis. From here it appeared to tower higher than its 166 km, set against the blue sky. He smiled and agreed that was the best spot. I took a favourable seat and gazed at the twisted, gnarled limestone rock across the bay on which the ancient temple stood. The limestone character of most of Greece provides the infinite number of caves which were, of course, much appreciated by smugglers down the years but also led to countless legends of nymphs, demons, gods and paths to the Underworld.

The waiter brought my coffee and I asked him if we were looking down on St. Paul's Bay. He suddenly seemed less bored and advised that St.Paul's Bay was further south, round the other side of the headland on which Lindos stands. He told me it was a very beautiful bay with a little chapel that was popular for weddings. We were apparently looking down on Pallas beach, no doubt so named after Pallas Athene, the virgin goddess worshipped on the island at least since the 10th century B.C. It would have been ironic if it had given way to the most energetic evangelist of one of the most patriarchal of religions. I asked the waiter if there was any record of St. Paul ever having visited the bay that bore his name although I knew he had stopped at Rhodes town on his way from Antioch to Neapolis in Thrace and then down to Kos and Miletus. This was his third missionary journey. The waiter told me his father had been a fisherman who had thought Paul's visit quite possible since sudden winds and storms could play havoc in these waters even for craft larger than what might have conveyed Paul. The Bay might have been a very welcome shelter but would not have been more than that. Paul was an evangelist after all, and no one would have been listening in St.Paul's Bay in those days.

As I left I was hailed by a couple of women from our group on their way downhill. They were Lindsay, a likeable, gregarious lady from Edinburgh and Cynthia, slightly younger, probably early 40s from a Nigerian family in

London, equally good company. They had invited me the previous evening to join them for a late-night visit to some of the local bars. I think they had been a little surprised when I accepted, more surprised when I got into the spirit of the dancing that followed. They told me they were on their way to find a panini for lunch and did I want to join them. I said I'd be pleased to join them but not for a panini which is not my idea of lunch. I explained that I had intended to take the path down to the extensive beach and see which of the many restaurants had fresh fish that appealed to me. They decided to come with me.

The beach at Lindos is long and very safe. It was heavily populated with bodies of many shapes, few of them athletic. It was obvious that some of the restaurants had the typical British tourist in mind when deciding on menus so they had little in the way of fresh fish. We walked round the circular bay till we came near the jetty from which small boats left, almost in the shadow of the towering Acropolis. We found three offering seafood which looked worth the trouble. I suggested the one that seemed to me to have the best view over the water and we settled in. Our waiter was lively, especially when I discussed the food in Greek. They had a grouper and a red snapper, both of which we liked so we decided to share the two among three. The waiter had a mischievous look in his eye during our conversation. At the end of it he spoke English to be sure my companions heard and understood.

"So what`s your secret that you can get beautiful young ladies to lunch with you?"

He smiled at my friends who looked amused.

"I find speaking Greek with a Scottish accent does it every time," I replied.

The day was warm and the views across the bay beautiful. I had good company and when the food came it was excellent. Life can be pleasant at such times.

On the way back up the hill we were hailed by a couple of the donkey handlers who were relaxing in a hollow in the rock. They cheerfully accepted that we had no wish to go to the Acropolis. However, if they had not called to us we would not have noticed that the hollow in which they were resting was in the form of a stone ship, carved out of the rock. One of the men, noticing our interest shouted : "Jump in and we`ll take you for a sail round the island."

I wanted to make a second visit to Rhodes town which was another bus trip of about half an hour. That was my aim for the following day. This was partly because I had simply liked the town on my first sight of it some years before. However, I also wanted to investigate a little further just which set of knights had settled here. I had perhaps too easily believed a guide on my first visit who had assured me the Knights Templar had moved there from Jerusalem and had built the old town which was now so impressive. I had reason to doubt that. I also wanted to have another look at the lovely Venetian harbour and decide whether it really was ridiculous that the Colossus of Rhodes could have stood astride it.

The bus station where we arrived is a very short walk from the old town. You go a little downhill towards the sea and turn right. On the very broad pavement you pass street artists and stalls of local ware, carvings and implements in olive wood, olive oil soap in countless different packagings and much more. The spot is favourable mainly because of the tourist traffic, but it is enhanced by the shade of a number of large trees. Across the road, beside the harbour, are very modern restaurants serving throughout the day. You then turn right and reach the magnificent entrance to the old town. Tall, crenellated round towers guard each side of the road. This fortified mediaeval area is built in a semicircle around the central harbour. It shows few signs of age, partly because the Italians who occupied the island in the early part of the twentieth century, gave a lot of attention to its restoration. You walk in along the pavement and soon find yourself in the splendid cobbled streets with the Palace of the Knights, the Archaeological Museum and, at the end of the Ippoton, the Palace of the Grand Masters.

These are all imposing buildings in pale stone. The Ippoton (avenue of knights) is a long, cobbled street lined by the `inns` for each of the `tongues`. Since the knights came from all over Europe each nationality had its own `inn`.

I went into the archaeological museum, primarily to get an answer to my question about which group of knights had actually occupied Rhodes. Were they the Knights Templar or were they the Knights of St. John, also known as The Knights Hospitaller. As far as I understand it, the Knights Templar were a military order founded to protect pilgrims going to the Middle East after the Islamic conquests. The Knights Hospitaller had been founded in Jerusalem to offer medical help to sick pilgrims. The immediate question on viewing the magnificent old town of Rhodes is how they could get so rich from opening hospitals. I went into the archaeological museum which is a splendid building in itself. This was apparently the 15th century knights `hospital. It has broad stone staircases, large, high-ceilinged rooms and a gallery on the upper floor, leading outside to a terrace with exhibits among shrubs and small trees.

There was an information desk and I addressed the young woman on duty. She listened carefully to my question, nodded and reached over to give me a sheet from the block of information handouts on the counter. The sheet had a map of the city and a few paragraphs down the side providing a brief run through the main landmarks in its history. Hardly the informed discussion I had hoped for.

I was not so single-minded about my question as to ignore the treasures of the museum. I began to stroll through its many rooms, looking at countless artefacts. The survival of pottery is often the most valuable source of information. Metal rusts or corrodes, paper disintegrates or burns. Pottery may shatter but the remnants survive. It was evident that from around at least the eighth century BC Rhodes was actively trading with Crete, Kos, Samothrace, Egypt, Turkey and mainland Greece. It is known that trade was probably occurring earlier, perhaps from around the fifteenth century BC but this was disrupted by waves of hostile invaders to the Eastern Mediterranean. Some stability seems to have taken hold from around the eighth century B.C. when the Dorians arrived. From then on you begin to see a major development in the quality of work. Much of the pottery is intricately decorated. Human figures become more expressive and detailed. This culminated in the beautiful kneeling statue of Aphrodite of Rhodes and, perhaps even more strikingly, in the famous Laokoon. This wonderful creation is now in the Vatican Museum in Rome, but Pliny the Elder records that it was created by Agesander in Rhodes. It has not proved possible to date Agesander, but the sculpture may have been done as early as the fourth century BC or could be as late as the first. It is not simply a decoration on a piece of kitchenware like so much of what went before it. It is a sculpture in the modern sense, but one that has scarcely ever been matched for quality. It depicts the fate of Laokoon who is mentioned in Homer`s Iliad. He was a Trojan priest of Poseidon. The unfortunate man warned his fellow citizens not to allow the Trojan horse into the city. Either for this challenge to the will of the gods or for some other misdemeanour like perhaps making love in the presence of a divine image he suffered a cruel fate. This, reportedly, was administered by Athena whom he had enraged. First of all, she blinded him. Then she sent two giant sea serpents to kill him and his sons. The great sculpture shows Laokoon struggling with the monsters as his sons look to him for help which he cannot give. It is not only the technical magnificence of the sculpture which is interesting. It is also a presentation of one of the insights of the ancient Greeks which is just as valid today. It resembles the myth of the titan, Prometheus, in showing an individual who dares to defy the gods. Perhaps the story of the death of Socrates belongs in the same category. People who stand out from the crowd even when motivated by the best aims often suffer for their individuality.

I went from this impressive building up the Ippoton, The Avenue of Knights, to reach another imposing structure. This is the Palace of the Grand Master. This spacious and sumptuous palace was restored by the Italians after an explosion of gunpowder in it in 1856 had left it a ruin. This was undertaken with a view to its being a holiday home for Mussolini and King Emmanuel III. The effect is certainly majestic, but doesn't give much indication of what it might have been like in the time of the Knights. However, here I was fortunate to find a young guide who was only too happy to air his knowledge of his town's history. He told me that it is probable that the knights who built these original structures were Knights Hospitaller. However, his own view was that the distinction between them on the one hand and the Knights Templar often became blurred. It seems certain that the Hospitallers whose aim was the provision of medical care had an effective military aspect. The Knights Templar whose role was intended to be largely military certainly became involved in other areas of life such as founding what was essentially the first banking system. This enabled intending pilgrims or crusaders in France, Italy or elsewhere, to deposit money in their home country and then draw on it in Jerusalem or Rhodes. The wealth of the Templars may have been their downfall in that they were owed large amounts of money by the Pope and the King of France in the early 13th century. Slaughtering them and destroying the order was thought by these august personages to be a better course of action than repaying anything. This did not happen to the Knights Hospitaller who survive to the present day in organisations such as St. John`s Ambulance Brigade.

If you move on from these palaces you reach the area known as The Hora. This is simply the Greek word for `country` or `stretch of land`. It is still within the walls of the old city but consists of endless shops, markets and restaurants. I find it a fascinating place to wander or sit and have coffee or beer. I had done my exploring and research and saw no likelihood of getting much closer to the truth about the knights who once occupied the island.

After idling for a time I went back out to the magnificent harbour. However you looked at it it seemed impossible that a statue could have stood astride it. It hardly needed the unanimous judgement of engineers to confirm this. Having said this, it seems very probable that the Colossus of Rhodes did exist. One quite credible tradition is that it came about as a result of an attack launched on it by the Macedonian general Demetrius whose nickname,Polyorcetes, means `besieger of cities`. Demetrius had a very colourful life including five marriages, countless battles and the kind of sexual extravagances which we regard as deviant but which appear to have been tediously normal for powerful leaders of Eastern Mediterranean lands. In 305 BC he launched an attack on Rhodes to punish the island for its having allied itself with his enemies in earlier wars. He appears to have been very ingenious in devising military equipment to achieve his aims. To deal with the high walls around Rhodes town he brought a structure called Helepolis which probably meant `city of the sun`. It was reportedly 38 metres high and required 3,000 men to haul it into position. Once there archers and other soldiers could climb it and get over the city walls. However, before he could complete his siege Demetrius was forced to withdraw by the arrival of his enemy Ptolemy, so abandoning his military equipment including the Helepolis. The Rhodians considered this an act of divine intervention and resolved to build a monument to Helios, the sun-god. They called on Chares of Lindos who had been involved in other huge structures to undertake the task. He e clad the Helepolis in bronze forming a human shape. The whole thing was not a very good idea in an earthquake zone and a severe tremor brought the huge structure crashing down in 226 BC. The gigantic remnants lay on the ground for centuries. There appears to be no certainty about the ultimate fate of them. One story is that they were sold to a Jew of Odessa who took them away on 900 camels. It seems likely that story was created by Arab invaders to bolster their disdain for Jews in general.

I took one more trip on this visit. There was a coach excursion around the southern half of the island, taking us to the west and south. I had no knowledge of that area so

I decided to go for it. Three of the ladies in our group decided on this one as well so we made our way in the early morning past the goats and down to the collection point. It was already very hot so we were pleased when the coach pulled up a little ahead of time. Our escort was the small Englishman I had come across earlier in the stay. Cheerful as he was, I realised we would not be supplied with much information, historical, linguistic or even gastronomic during the day. On the other hand, I expected that we would be exposed to every possible opportunity to buy alcohol.

In fact our first stop was not alcohol related. We had only travelled 20 minutes north of Lindos when we passed Feraklos Castle on the coast to our right. It stands in the little coastal village of Haraki. Our escort told us it had been built by the Italians to defend the island from the Turks. This is almost certainly wrong. It is known that it was used by the Knights of St. John in the 1300's but was an existing fortification before then, possibly begun by the Byzantines, occasionally used by pirates. The Knights extensively renovated it and did indeed use it to defend against Turkish raids. However, it was eventually taken by the troops of Suleiman the Magnificent in 1522 since he had good reason to believe the Knights were harbouring one of his great enemies. This led to the departure of the Knights from Rhodes to take up residence in Malta.

However, our stop was not actually at Feraklos Castle. We pulled up at a battered little shed which turned out to be an olive oil bottling plant. Inside it looked much larger and better maintained than we had expected. A young lady gave us a brief rundown in reasonable English of the many processes required to turn the unpleasant fruit which is a natural olive into this wonderful product which has so many uses in cooking and cosmetics. Then she began to describe the work of the bottling plant. It`s not a subject of compelling interest to me, important as it is, but I found myself getting gradually irritated by a man`s voice amongst our group, constantly muttering something. I looked round and saw a middle-aged man with spectacles saying something to his small wife. I conquered my initial annoyance and concluded he perhaps had a good reason and, really, he was not doing a lot of harm.

We got back on the bus and I noticed the muttering man and his wife were in the seats in front of me. I chatted to Debbie sitting next to me for a while and then realised the small English escort was having some kind of difficult conversation with the muttering man. I should explain that the escort had a strong East London accent. The escort noticed my taking an interest and said "The gentleman has asked about Lord Byron and I`m trying to remember where he died." "He died of a fever in Missolonghi" I replied. "Ah!" said the little man "Now how do I explain to this foreign gentleman that Byron wanted to fight for the Greeks against the Turks but not in Rhodes?" I asked the muttering man where he was from and he replied "Belgium". So, hoping he was a Walloon rather than Fleming I spoke to him in French whereupon he smiled and began to talk enthusiastically. The little escort shrugged and good-humouredly said "If only I`d know I`d have saved my braincells." I immediately realised the man had been muttering to his wife because she spoke no English at all and he had been trying to translate for her. I also realised that his English was not great and the strong accent of our escort was an additional hurdle. Immediately I felt ashamed of my annoyance. English speakers are of course pampered the world over so why should he not help his wife to understand when they had come so far?

The coach went on past Archangelosk, the third largest population centre on the island. The people there have the reputation of being very individual with a dialect of their own and keeping to some of the traditional customs and cuisine of the island. It has apparently expanded a lot in recent times but the old village is said to be well preserved. Since we didn`t stop at it I assumed it was not known for its alcohol production.

We then turned off the coast road that leads to Rhodes town. The interior is sparsely populated and densely wooded. From time to time the thick forest covering gave way to some farmland and small villages. As in so much of Greece there appeared to be one church for every member of the population. I wondered if every announcement of a pregnancy led to a fever of church-building. Perhaps they had a standard design for what could be built in nine months. I`d like to have known more about these little communities and how well they fared in the modern world. Did all the young people leave for the towns or foreign parts? Did wealthy Greeks and others come and buy houses as second homes? How much had the traditional life changed? If our escort knew any of these things he was not inclined to tell us. I contrasted this with the extravagant outpouring of information I`d experienced in Crete from Elias, the rotund fount of endless facts about every settlement we passed.

Eventually we arrived at a winery near Embonas which is the main wine-producing area on the island. I had visited this before and have little interest in wine in the late morning. However, I quickly discovered that I could sit outside in the shade and be served some excellent coffee. Most of the party bundled in with great eagerness. The description of the wine-making process is quite interesting but why people should be so eager to buy there and then, sometimes in quantity, amazes me. Wine is not rare after all. We have an abundance of it in shops all over Europe and beyond.

I was sitting enjoying my coffee and reading a local newspaper when I noticed the Belgians wandering out a little disconsolately. I invited them to join me and advised that the brew was quite acceptable. When they sat down they explained to me that they rarely drank wine. Their country is, after all, famous for producing more than 400 different beers. They confirmed that was their preferred tipple, especially in the heat we were experiencing. The wife became quite animated now and I realised what a torment it must have been to her to be unable to communicate with anyone other than her husband. I asked what had made them choose Rhodes. She explained that they had seen something of neighbouring European countries in their occasional holidays and wanted to visit somewhere quite different. I asked if Rhodes was living up to expectations. The husband nodded vigorously. The wife explained that it was in the main. They were a little frustrated at the poor range of beers available. I agreed with this but it`s not uncommon in southern Europe. Most in my experience conformed to a type of pleasant but characterless lager which was refreshing on a hot day. In general they liked the food although one or two meals had disappointed. They thought the island beautiful and interesting and the inhabitants friendly. That largely was my own opinion. They also agreed that the coffee we were having was really quite good.

We soon set off again after I sat watching couples who had seemed to have some difficulty walking into the winery stumbling out with remarkable quantities of wine, labouring in the hot sunshine to stow their treasure safely on the bus. The driver opened the boot and watched with, I thought, a flicker of incredulity as these portly passengers wheezed and heaved their packages into safety.

Our next stop soon after was in the village of Embonas and it was time for lunch. It is a settlement of just over 1,000 inhabitants and its prosperity is largely based on wine. The coach stopped in a small square and our guide pointed to the chosen restaurant. In we went to see an interior the size of a small concert hall with tables and chairs going on and on. A tall, very overweight, quite depressed- looking young man wearily extended an arm to show us where to sit. He needn`t have bothered since it was the only table that was set and was long enough for all of us. An older, smaller woman stood at the back watching. She could not match the size and weight of the younger waiter but she seemed to share equally in his gloom. We were so accustomed to smiling welcomes in Rhodes that we were surprised. I briefly wondered if this was a waiting-room for the damned in some Homeric legend. Helios, the sun-god who was the resident deity of the island, had surely never made an appearance here. The young man lumbered off as the woman remained, gimlet- eyed, alert to any signs of escape or flight. Eventually the young man ambled back carrying jugs of wine. He was followed by a smaller, older man with a white moustache and receding grey hair. The lines around his eyes suggested he had once smiled but, we felt, might not do so again. He too brought wine as if in apology for the awfulness of the mood.

The Belgian couple decided to try the local vintage and their faces immediately suggested this was a gloom-inducing potion. Life appeared to drain from their eyes as they peered into a Stygian abyss. Then they looked at us and we all laughed. I wondered when that had last happened within these sad walls. In short, the meal was dreadful. Anonymous, cold meat was surrounded by tepid rice and a few beans. At least there was reasonable pitta bread and some houmous and tsatziki that were edible. On emerging I collared our escort and told him clearly that that was by far the worst meal I had tasted in many trips to Greece. The Belgians, possibly understanding my tone more than my words, nodded vehemently in agreement. The little Englishman frowned with affected concern and said he would have to report that. I think his report was probably not the only one nor the most damning.

We trundled on, now travelling down the west coast. Although picturesque, the weather on this side is much less predictable than on the Lindos side. For that reason there are fewer habitations along it, but eventually we entered a little town called Siana which, our escort explained, held a special treat for us. As the coach trundled through it I noticed neat small houses in different colours from stone-grey to ochre. I saw gardens and a striking church. I wondered if we were indeed to see something memorable. We were, by now, not necessarily impressed by his taste in such matters but we were curious. The bus stopped on the narrow main road and we piled out onto the pavement. The little escort breezily led us uphill but our destination was none of the interesting scenes we had passed. It was a café. After the dreadful lunch I was not necessarily averse to finding something edible, but I doubted if that was the aim. In we went to a simple place with wooden tables and chairs. My eye was caught immediately by letters and postcards pinned to the walls and doors, received from far and wide in a multitude of languages. The owner clearly had made an impression. However, my heart sank a little as I saw the expected table in the centre with lots of small liqueur glasses filled with, of course, souma,the local grappa. The idea was to taste it and then rush up to the counter at the back and buy as many bottles as you could afford. I bypassed this display and went up to a woman standing by the counter and asked her if she had anything to eat. She looked a little surprised but said they had some spinach pie. Ideal. I asked if I could have some along with a coffee and could I have it on the little terrace outside which looked out over dense trees and flowering plants down to a small beach and the deep blue sea. She agreed and I was joined in this by some of the others equally indifferent to souma.

 Since I finished this little snack well before the coach was due to set off again I decided to stroll along the main street to see if Siana had anything else to offer. I particularly wanted a closer look at the church. I was accompanied by Jennie and Debbie from our party. It was a beautifully warm, sunny afternoon so a stroll in the fresh air was welcome even if there was nothing to see. However, we soon discovered that there was very much something to see and we wondered at the quality of the escort who had not bothered to mention it to us. To our left was a neat row of shops which suggested we had reached the centre of the little village. Some steps went down from the pavement on our right to an open, paved area in which sat one of the most beautiful churches I have ever seen. This was Agios Pantoleimon which means `holy forgiveness`. The main entrance had a black wrought-iron gate. Around it was a high arch in white-painted stone, contrasting with the pale green of the wall around it. Above the arch were three stained glass windows with the panels outlined delicately in white. On either side of the entrance was a rectangular clock tower which rose well above the roof of the main part of the church. They narrowed a little at the top to become bell towers topped with a trinity of little rectangular pillars, one large and two small. Each was black-capped with a small blue cross on top. Rising above the black pitched roof a little back from the entrance was a circular section with a black domed roof. In this section were tall, narrow stained –glass windows like the ones above the entrance. Inside, the effect was dazzling. Chandeliers and rood screens in silver and gold surrounded us and the ceiling was rich with paintings of Bible scenes in lemon yellow, ochre and orange. Above the rood screen was a row of icons of saints. It is not, I think, generally realised that these icons are highly stylised, so that the image of St. Matthew, for example, in Rhodes will be the same as that in Crete, or Samos or mainland Greece. That reinforces the specialness of the word `iconic` which is used so glibly in journalistic writing. We stood drenched in this symphony of colour that was almost audible and wondered at the care, the artistry and, indeed, the expense of such a special place of worship. I wondered if our fellow passengers with their souma could be as intoxicated as we now felt by this amazing scene.

We came out again to the strong sunlight outside. Beside the church was a tall acacia tree with masses of purple flowers. Suddenly we noticed among these blooms a large butterfly with wings striped in red and yellow. This natural scene was as captivating as the man-made one inside. We all took out our cameras but the little insect`s deftness at avoiding photography suggested he`d had a past-life as a Hollywood star accustomed to dodging paparazzi We all ran around, bumping into one another, no doubt to the great entertainment of our target.

We climbed aboard again congratulating ourselves on finding treasures we would have missed if we had simply followed our escort. I noticed the heavy eyelids and flushed faces of some of our fellows who had been a little too enthusiastic about the local brews. The day was wearing on and some of their excesses were beginning to show.

We were now quite far south on the island and the road went on, scenic but with few habitations or settlements. Eventually we reached our next goal which was Prasonisi. This is the southernmost part of Rhodes. The name means `green island` and refers to what is, for much of the time, an island. At other times when the sea recedes somewhat there is a sandy causeway which leads to it. In fact we did not go as far as the island. We were allowed an hour to walk on the wide, clean beach, sit in one of the cafés or take our chances running across the causeway. Jennie and Debbie and I opted for a café on the sand, looking out to the sea and the small island. I had a beer and we began to talk about music. Debbie`s main interest was her church choir. Jennie liked soul music and old-fashioned rock. I stood up for opera and Tony Bennett. We debated folk music and agreed that the term was far too elastic. We could all think of examples of it we could happily enjoy and others we`d switch off. I got no support for the opera suggestion until they agreed that the duet on the old British Airways advert was great and that is the Flower Song from Lakmé by Delibes. We reached total agreement that labels for music were not helpful. Saying you love or hate any category is probably untrue. There`s just good music and bad music.

We returned to the bus and sat largely in silence as we turned north towards Lindos. Gentle snoring was audible from those who had imbibed and we had all exhausted most of our conversation. A little later I and the nine ladies went out with Emma, our rep, to a rooftop restaurant where, in the dying light we could just make out the Acropolis as the hills around us began to show more and more lights. The restaurant was spacious and friendly and the food was very good. My thoughts largely drifted as the ladies discussed their views on the fashion for shoulder-pads and whether some journalist writing for *Vogue* was really ahead of fashion or years behind it. The air was warm and pleasant after the fiery heat of the day. I reflected on how much I liked this island despite the minor inconveniences of a rather ill-chosen holiday company.

MY SECOND VISIT TO CRETE

When I am in Greece, whether mainland or islands, I often have a sense that visitors are very welcome to enjoy the sunshine, the excellent seafood and the spectacular scenery, but are unlikely to share in a timeless world that goes on behind or beyond all of that. I`m almost ashamed to confess it but at times in Greece I can`t help thinking of Pythagoras who, in addition to making observations about the hypotenuse of a right-angled triangle also claimed to be able to hear the music of the spheres. It`s odd that if someone in your local pub made such a claim you`d probably suggest he`d had one beverage too many. With Pythagoras the statement was recorded for future generations to wonder at. He had   obviously built up some credibility with his geometrical discoveries, but on the other hand warned disciples not to eat beans since they contained the transmigrated souls of one`s ancestors. This might seem to undermine his status as a sage but perhaps it was simply a delicate way of warning against flatulence. In any event, in Greece I have more often than anywhere else had the strange feeling that another life was going on beyond any that I could see. If the music of the spheres was going to be heard anywhere then it would be here. Given that I have never visited

119

Pythagoras` native island of Samos nowhere has this feeling been stronger than in Crete.

Crete is by far the largest of the Greek islands and also the most southerly. Some say it is the most beautiful but I can`t confirm that. I haven`t seen all of the islands and I haven`t seen all of Crete. There has been considerable beauty in all of the ones I`ve visited and all I can say is that in my experience Crete is certainly no exception. Its situation in the southern part of the Eastern Mediterranean means it has been influenced greatly by Egypt and Phoenicians in ancient times and later by more or less hostile attentions from Romans, Turks, Venetians, Britain (as a protectorate) and most recently and most horrifyingly, by Nazi Germany. Oddly, it was hardly touched by the intellectual flowering of Classical Greece and was entirely bypassed by expansionist Persians and the Macedonian empire of Alexander the Great. In some ways its most interesting and significant historical period was before any of these empires in the wonderful civilisation of the people known to us as Minoans who flourished in the region until the devastating explosion of Thera around 1500 BC. We`ll return to that theme.

In June 2013 I joined a group who were heading for Crete. It was the kind of group I had been with several times before. I knew none of the party but the format suited me. I could have company at breakfast and dinner if I

wanted and there were some excursions on offer but I
was free to go about on my own as much as I wanted. Our
hotel was in Iolida, near Agia Marina, on the north coast
just a few miles from Chania which I had heard described
as the most beautiful town in Crete. I had been to the
island before with my friend Suzie, but at that time we
had stayed in Stalidas which is more than 60 miles further
east.

Our hotel in Iolida was modern, clean and comfortable
with very fine views out to the sea and inland to some of
the high mountains. We had arrived quite early and I
decided to get a flavour of the town. It was mid afternoon
and I walked in pleasant sunshine with a temperature in
the upper 20s. It wasn`t long before I came to a
reasonable-looking taverna. It had no walls or windows as
such on two sides, simply very thick wooden pillars
supporting a ceiling whose heavy, dark beams formed a
kind of trellis for vines and bougainvillea to twist their way
through. The one wall on my right as I looked at it from
the road had a large mural of blue sea, sand and hills with
a worldly -looking curly-haired god lounging on a beach
offering wine to a couple of shapely nymphs who could
have been goddesses or possibly British tourists. It looked
shaded and welcoming in a warm afternoon so I went in.
No one appeared at first but I was happy enough to watch
people stroll past. Eventually a man came out, obviously
intending to set some tables for later. He was slim and a

little round-shouldered with dark hair. He had a look of worry on his face which appeared to be permanent, not the result of any particular concern, just a general reaction to life. He came over to me without the usual Greek welcoming smile. I said "Good Day" in Greek and explained that I would like some beer and perhaps something light to eat. He stared at me as if I'd asked him for a heart transplant. Then, after a moment's thought which appeared to cause him serious difficulty, he replied. I couldn't understand a word of what he said. I repeated my request. He looked equally troubled and held up his hand as if to tell me not to move. Then he disappeared. I felt a little discouraged both at my Greek not being understood and at having no idea what language he had used for the reply. After a few moments a woman came out. She was perhaps forty, a little overweight, but pleasant-looking apart from a similar look of worry. She asked me in German if she could help me. I asked her in German why she was speaking to me in German since I was Scottish and could speak Greek. She looked puzzled and explained "Stavros" had said I was German. I asked why he had thought that since I had addressed him in Greek. I repeated the request in Greek. She smiled and shook her head. Evidently she understood me and wrote my order down. I asked what language Stavros had used for the reply. She shrugged her shoulders a little and said "That was Stavros speaking English." I took it from the way she said it that Stavros` excursions into English often resulted in confusion.

I walked the short distance back to the hotel where a welcoming drink was on offer along with details of excursions we could take. Then we went for dinner in the hotel dining room. I spent some time talking to a large Englishman named Ian and two ladies, Kim and Sue, who sat opposite us. I was reassured that I was amongst likeable people. I assumed, however, that their interest in Crete would be a little different from mine. I was accustomed to companions who mainly wanted to sunbathe and sample the drinks on offer. I didn`t object to that but my interests were different. Agia Marina itself is pleasant. It is not much more than a main street with restaurants and cafés but it is only 6 miles from Chania.

Since nothing was planned for our first full day on Crete I decided to take the local bus into Chania. I enjoy bus journeys abroad. It makes me feel much more a part of the place than would be possible in a hired car. I`m always struck by the fact that there is never any indication on buses anywhere of how one is supposed to pay for the journey. Sometimes you see a machine into which a ticket should be inserted but usually no explanation of how the ticket is to be obtained. On the bus to Chania there was no machine and the driver showed no interest in who had boarded or left the bus. Nor did I see warnings such as I have seen in, for example, Australia or Singapore, of the many transgressions which can lead to fines from the modest to the entire life savings of the Rothschilds. No ticket, expired ticket, eating, drinking, smoking talking to the driver, putting feet on the seats or even on the metal support around the seats, bringing pets or allowing pets to eat the passengers, displaying hostility or, worse, showing needless affection were severely forbidden in such places. As far as I could see on the bus to Chania nothing was forbidden, nor anything expected, including payment. Everyone, including a careworn bloodhound, sat quietly without feet on seats or eating or drinking. No one was smoking, singing, fighting or engaging in intimacy. Eventually we stopped at a small village where a woman in a uniform came on with a ticket machine over one shoulder and a holder of different coin denominations over another. She moved swiftly through the bus knowing with uncanny perceptiveness who had tickets and who not. She stopped beside me and raised an enquiring eyebrow. I said "Chania" and held out a 5 euro note. She took the money, gave me a ticket and dispensed my change.

The bus station in Chania sits in a busy part of the city, uphill from the sea in Plateia Kalaidi. It wasn`t obvious to me which road I should take for the harbour which I wanted to visit. However, I knew that it would be downhill and I decided to stroll along for a time and simply absorb the atmosphere. I walked along Kydonias which is a busy throughfare that forms the northern edge of the bus station. It was busy in the pleasant Greek way which I have noticed in several parts of the country. Although people were doing things they showed no stress or pressure. If they met a friend they stopped to chat. If they passed a market they looked at its products carefully. As I reached a major junction with traffic lights I came to a fish shop on my right. Fish shops abroad always interest me. They usually have much more on offer than you find in their Scottish equivalents. That of course is partly a reflection of the different species available in the local sea. I looked at the slabs and identified Tuna, squid, octopus, salmon, whitebait and prawns. Others had names I did not recognise and have been unable to find in dictionaries. *Gopes* looked to me like sea bream. There was one called *Sabridia*, about the size of sea bass but more elongated. It is, of course, quite possible that these were local Cretan names since it has strong dialect variations from mainland Greek.

I saw a sign to the town centre and took it. It led downhill so I was confident I was going the right way. That led me soon to the broad thoroughfare named Eleftherios Venizelos. This name is famous in Crete and throughout Greece. He was the talented and visionary politician who, more than anyone, deserves to be called the founder of modern Greece. He was born in August 1864 and became a leader in his native Crete and then brought his island into union with Greece in 1897 after long and bloody confrontations with the Ottoman Turks trying desperately to hold onto the tatters of their once-mighty empire. The Turks had no choice but to give way once the `great powers`, Britain, France, Russia and Italy supported the Venizelos programme. He was a liberal and a democrat and was hotly opposed in Greece by the monarchists, particularly in the First World War where he moved against strong opposition to ally Greece with Britain and France. He served his country as Prime Minister several times between 1910 and his death in 1933.

When I reached this broad street I was immediately facing the market square. If I walked a little to where the road intersected with Andrea Papandreou there was what looked like an inviting, modern café. It was around 11 in the morning so I was ready for my `fix`. I was also curious. In some parts of Greece cafés are a little primitive and have this peculiar offering which is Nescafé with evaporated milk squirted into it. It reminds me of my early childhood when we had food rationing in Britain after the war. Quality coffee was rare and sometimes milk was as well. Indeed even poor quality coffee was rare and strange preparations of chicory and dandelion root were promoted as being excellent substitutes. I prefer not to relive these days. By contrast, in Rhodes town, Parga, Athens and the island of Levkas I have found some of the most stylish and inviting places where I have been able to enjoy a very high quality Americano, as good as I could expect in London, Edinburgh or New York. From that list I should not omit Melbourne, Australia, which has some of the most consistently good coffee I have tasted. I don`t go for other versions such as latte, skinny latte, Mocha and only rarely espresso, but they were on offer also. I went in and the clientele were mostly well-dressed young Greeks. After having seen and read so much about the country`s economic hardships it was difficult to reconcile what I knew to be the truth about their national finances with a scene of affluence. I have seen this paradox played out again and again in different parts of the country.

After my scene of multi-lingual miscommunication the day before in Agia Marina I was a little hesitant about speaking Greek again but I knew I had to try, like horse riders after being thrown who feel they must get immediately back in the saddle or they`ll never ride again. Neat-looking young waitresses were busy as I looked in vain for a seat. I stopped one long enough to establish that there was more space upstairs. I went up and sat in a cool, modern booth overlooking the market square. I assumed it would be a while before anyone came to serve me but I was wrong. Almost immediately a young waitress, looking relaxed and unflustered turned up. Then she made my day by allowing me to greet her and order in Greek. This drew a wider smile and a little `bravo`. Even better, she answered me in Greek rather than feeling the need to display her English which was probably very good.

Now, caffeine-replenished, I set off again, deciding that Chania was a nice place to be even if it did not turn out to be the beautiful spot I had read about. I continued across the market square and soon got my first glimpse of the sea. A further short walk took me to the harbour, a wide, almost circular bay with just a narrow opening to the Mediterranean. The Venetians, perennial rivals of the Ottomans, who once occupied the island, had obviously prized this natural bay and had enhanced it to be one of the most beautiful areas imaginable. It fully matched my expectations. The deep blue water sparkled, surrounded almost totally by a broad, elegantly paved area in pale stone. I have read that the entire island of Crete is a nightmare for boats of any size. In all of this large island there are only around three acceptable harbours of which Chania is the best. It`s no surprise therefore that the Venetians who occupied the island and gave this town its modern name lavished care on it.

 I walked down to the front. The sun was warm but not ferocious. On either side of me were cafés and restaurants round more than half of the circle of the bay. On my right, on the eastern side a stone walkway went on beyond the tavernas to a lighthouse almost straight ahead of me at the narrow outlet to the sea. Presumably this harbour was the reason the settlement has been important since the earliest times. Under its old name, Kydonia, it was important in the Minoan world.

That great civilisation began perhaps around 3,000 BC and demonstrated taste and culture along with commercial success until the collapse around 1500 BC. Whether that was entirely a result of the huge explosion of Thera to the north or invasion by the crude Mycenaeans has never been established. That civilisation also produced the first coded laws in Greek history. The Law of Gortys was discovered in different sections on the site of that name by French and, later, German archaeologists in the later 19th century. It is surprisingly liberal and civilised in its provisions with, for example, far more sane protection for the rights of women than exists in most subsequent codes, whether theological or secular. Advocates of various religious and philosophical belief systems like to suggest their particular creed has been essential to the preservation of public morals. The Law of Gortys suggests the world of the Minoans did not need any lessons in public behaviour from the bloodthirsty and bigoted tribes that followed. So Kydonia was perhaps the most important settlement of that ancient culture along with Gortys itself, Knossos and Phaestos. Homer was aware of the great culture on Crete and, much later, so was Plato. Even after the disasters of the Thera explosion and the Mycenean invasion it recovered to achieve eminence even in Roman and later Byzantine times.

I decided to walk round to the lighthouse, a distance of about 1.5 miles from where I stood. On the way I could look closely at the various eating places and give them a chance to impress me with what they had available. It was now after mid-day and the sun was warm. I walked past open-air restaurants under awnings to provide shade and saw some geared to the tourist taste for burgers, chips and beer and, further on, smaller, plainer ones offering freshly caught fish, probably grilled in oil or butter and served with salad and perhaps rice. I continued and the promenade opened out to a broad, paved area where horse-drawn carriages waited for business. It reminded me of a piazza in Florence, designed by someone who was aware that life was about much more than the heat of battle. It suggested a civilised mentality that knew that citizens should have space and elegance in which to enjoy the sunshine, the blue sea and strolling with friends. Perhaps they would be heading for an evening meal in the open by the blue water of the bay, just darkening as the sun began to set out beyond the lighthouse. Beside the carriages was a former mosque, now used as a tourist information centre. Both the mosque and the paving were in the pale limestone that gives such an impression of cleanness and light in the Greek sun.

I continued along the sea wall towards the lighthouse and found myself behind a couple of sturdy English ladies walking side by side. The walkway was narrow and I could not pass. The delay was a little frustrating but it did enable me to discover that a certain type of ladies` shoe could be purchased more cheaply in Barnsley than was possible in Rochdale, although the range of sizes was slightly greater in the latter. I had to accept that if the ladies had been weak-willed and susceptible to the distraction of the loveliest harbour in Crete or even the elementary courtesy of not blocking the narrow path then I`d never have gained this insight into footwear issues for the urban female with no obvious dress sense. After a few minutes we came to a stairway which led up to a higher level of the wall, presumably once vital when watching for enemy shipping. The ladies showed no interest in enemy shipping and I was able to climb the stairs, walk smartly along the upper walkway and back down ahead of them as they broadened their intensive study to include the range of colours one might consider in Barnsley. I was able to continue on to the lighthouse. From there I looked back admiringly at the almost circular bay. I do not have the expertise to determine how much the effect came from a wonderful natural setting and how much praise was due to the Italian designers or subsequent Cretan additions, but the effect was very pleasing. Amid the Italianate buildings and others I took to be Cretan in design there was the occasional minaret and Islamic dome that added to the exotic effect. In the distance was a skyline of high mountains which probably play a part in this sense that another world is going on in the island.

I had mentally selected a restaurant on my way past as my first choice for lunch if it had something worthwhile on offer. It was small, slightly set back from the others and had made few concessions to décor or gloss. It only had about eight tables under a blue awning and the only customer was an old sea dog sitting with a small carafe of wine and one sardine on a plate. He was chatting to the waiter, a man in his early forties wearing a white shirt and unremarkable dark trousers. They both looked at me as I walked in. There was no hostility in their glance but it was the look they would have given someone expected to ask for directions to the British pub. Perhaps they had already given just such directions to a couple of women from Barnsley. It was far from the fawning servility of waiters competing for the tourist market. I asked in Greek if the restaurant was open for lunch. I saw in the waiter`s eyes the initial confusion I often saw of not understanding me until he realised I was speaking Greek. Then there was a little smile and the word `vevaios` which means `certainly`. I then asked if he had fresh fish and he smiled more broadly and repeated the same word with more emphasis. I asked if I could see what was on offer. I then got the treatment I would never expect in any British restaurant. He invited me to come into the kitchen and see what was fresh. He had the usual sea bream and sea bass. There was an eel which was tempting. I had eaten eel in Morocco and had been surprised at how good it had been. Then there was an octopus. I had eaten tiny octopus in Spain but never one this size. Its body was a little larger than my hand and the tentacles more than doubled that size. He saw me looking at it. He told me it had been caught the previous night and should be excellent. I told him I was hesitant since I had never eaten one like that. Of course I was not going to be offered, nor would I have welcomed, the whole thing, but it looked tough and muscular. He suggested I try it and then made the bold offer that if I didn`t like it he would not charge me for it. I accepted. I took my seat under the awning, looking out at the bay. I had once read Lawrence Durrell on a visit to the island of Chios witnessing a local woman whacking an octopus against a wall to tenderise it. I preferred not to consider whether my lunch had been subjected to wall-whacking. He brought me some white wine, bread and a couple of dishes, one of olive paste and one of garlic butter. Whilst uncertain whether my choice was wise I definitely felt I was abroad, in Greece, and I liked that feeling. The old sea dog eyed me for a bit and then asked where I was from. I told him I came from Scotland. He weighed this up for a bit and then asked me if I had a Greek wife. He asked in the way he might have asked if I had ever tasted the local wine, thinking to offer me some, but I decided he was not about to offer me a Greek wife. He was simply wondering why I spoke his language. I told him I didn`t have a Greek wife and he seemed to lose interest in the conversation. My octopus arrived. I tackled it with some trepidation but it was tender, succulent and tasty. I felt my boldness had been rewarded. I declined a dessert since I didn`t want to lose the satisfaction of the main course. Nonetheless, the waiter did not hesitate to bring me some baklava, a strong coffee and a small glass of what I took to be the local tsikoudia, a liqueur made in the wine-making process. On the mainland it is usually called tsipouro and it is sometimes referred to by the oriental name, raki.

I was pleased with my outing on my first day but did not want to return without seeing the excavations at the old city of Kydonias. That was only a short walk from where I sat with my octopus and after lunch I walked round. This is the ancient settlement round which the modern city has grown. Legend has it that it was founded by King Cydon, a son of the god Hermes. Whilst I could not prove this family connection was untrue it seemed to me to be as probable as the genealogy of Anglian and Saxon kings in old England, all of whom were descended from Odin. I suppose one has to credit gods with remarkable virility, but I wondered if these genealogies might have been trimmed a little if DNA testing had been around. I was full of admiration for Robert Pashley who had been the first to identify the location of the old city purely from literature, rather as Schliemann did when correctly locating Troy from his knowledge of Homer. Pashley was a fellow of Trinity Cambridge, distinguished in mathematics and classics. He had a travelling fellowship and visited Crete in the 1830s. I`ve no idea what literature led him to this conclusion but it was accurate. Also like Schliemann he was one of these 19$^{th}$ century polymaths. With his background in mathematics, classics and then whatever we call the skill of spotting ancient sites from poetry he wrote a couple of books on the `dismal science` of economics. Unfortunately not much has actually been excavated of the ancient city of Kydonia. Artefacts which have been unearthed can be seen in the Chania Archaeological museum, a beautiful building constructed by the Venetians, first used by Franciscan monks and later used as a mosque, then an arsenal, a cinema and finally the modern, elegant museum.

I returned to the hotel feeling my first day had been fruitful. Nonetheless, I felt that I had only opened the door a crack In Chania and would certainly return, probably the following day. So, I did return the following day but I was not alone. A little group of my fellow guests were intrigued by my adventure and decided to accompany me. We all piled on the local bus after breakfast. Having apparently given the impression that I was now familiar with every catering establishment and historic site in the city I sat on the bus wondering if I could find my way back from the bus station to the bay. There was only one other male in our small group and I assumed the ladies would soon fall victim to the many colourful shops in the town. After all, it was again almost time for my morning coffee and felt the others may not be so easily distracted by caffeine from exploring the city. As it happened, they were all ready for morning coffee and were impressed, as I had been, by the style, the service and the coffee of the place I led them to. I had a little hesitation in ordering in Greek since it was too obviously like showing off. However, a major aim of my trips to Greece is to increase my familiarity with this difficult language so if it seemed like needless ostentation then I would have to accept that. In fact, it drew another charming smile from the young waitress and immediately cemented my status as the guru of all things Hellenic. The reality of course is that each addition to my knowledge about the Greek world, ancient and modern, simply underlines how little I know.

After coffee the group split up a little. However, I walked around with Ian, Kim and Sue. As far as I could tell we actually had little in common but were immediately comfortable as a group. I wanted to explore the large covered market in the square across from the café and they joined me. We were all, I think, a little taken aback when we entered. The hall is enormous and full of stalls selling fish, wine, cheese, fruit, olive oil products and much else. Although covered, there was a sense of light and space which made it all the more pleasant to stroll amongst the many stalls. I have been in lots of covered markets over the years but this was the first one I have come across which seemed to me to compare with La Boqueria, the wonderful market off Ramblas in Barçelona. Increasingly, as we went round, we wondered what this large hall had originally been built for. I asked a couple of stall holders who were chatting in one of the aisles. They explained that it had been designed specifically as a covered market in 1911. The elder of the two pointed out that it had been built in the form of a cross, a fact we had not taken in, and part of the old Venetian city wall had had to be destroyed to build it. "You can`t eat history", he insisted, as if I were disagreeing with him. "After this was built you didn`t have to go all over the island to find what you wanted. People didn`t have cars. Now producers in the hills or in the villages can show their wares to the world." I thanked them for the information. They also thanked me although I was not sure what I had provided for them other than an opportunity to be enthusiastic.

We emerged again at the other end of the hall into the warm sun and a pedestrianised area full of cafés, shops and eating places. This is the broad street called Tsouderon. We turned left and enjoyed the scene. I had rarely seen a town that looked so prosperous and yet the atmosphere was relaxed. We felt no hustle or pressure to buy. I had suggested we gradually make our way down to the bay and choose a good place for lunch since that had been part of my plan if I had come back alone. We turned right down Episkopou Krisanthou and passed camera shops and a very visible tattoo and piercing studio. Kim spotted a stall with a basket of leaves and what looked like little balls of cotton wool. On inspection we noticed that some of the balls of cotton wool, actually more cylinders than balls, were moving and greedily eating the leaves. "I didn`t know you had to feed cotton wool," observed Ian. Our curiosity was satisfied when we looked at the shop behind the stall, displaying beautiful silk tablecloths, scarves and clothing. This was the first time any of us had ever seen silkworms.

The lady who owned the shop came out with a smile to talk to us. I didn`t know the Greek for silk or silkworms so she obligingly educated me about that to begin with. In fact I was in the market for a slightly unusual gift for my daughter. Dainty and stylish as she is she was representing the UK in the world powerlifting championships in Russia. She was doing well and I felt a silk item might mark the occasion appropriately. The others were equally intrigued. Apparently silk production has been established in Crete and other parts of Greece for more than a thousand years. Of course the amazing property of these little creatures was discovered in China around 2,700 BC. The story goes that the Empress Si-Lin-Chi was having a refreshing brew of tea in her garden when a cocoon fell into her cup. With the effect of the hot liquid out came a strong thread, providing the world with silk. The Chinese were not fond of exporting their discoveries it seems and Byzantine monks had to use subterfuge, hiding silkworms and leaves in their staffs to bring the discovery to Europe. I have no idea what kind of staffs were supplied to monks in those early days but it does sound suspiciously like KGB issue, designed for the stealthy transport of secrets rather than anything to be employed by unworldly evangelists. Perhaps that`s one reason why we use the adjective `Byzantine` to describe whatever is not quite what it seems. Industrial espionage is clearly not new. Robert Pashley reported from his visit to Crete in the 1830s that silk production and export were on a substantial scale. Also on a substantial scale was the smuggling of it to avoid the 3% tax on exporters.

At the time I was making this visit to Crete I was reading "The Colossus of Maroussi" by the American writer, Henry Miller. Miller, of course, became famous, or notorious, for his erotic accounts such as "Tropic of Cancer". His books have always struck me as the work of a man with a lot to say and a burning desire to be a writer but without much talent. "The Colossus of Maroussi" was supposed to be about the Greek poet George Katsoumbalis but is mostly a rant about how much more wonderful life is in Greece than in the USA. His view of the subject was probably heavily influenced by his resentment at being called up for military service in 1941 but he came to mind as I was strolling around Chania with new friends and anticipating an excellent lunch by the sea. Miller said "The light of Greece opened my eyes, penetrated my pores, expanded my whole being." Whilst I think his native country has far more to offer than he allowed I agree that Greece has a special charm and Chania displays it admirably.

We all spent some money in the silk shop and then strolled through some of the older, less commercial streets to the bay. My friends were as enchanted by the sight as I had been and eagerly agreed to walk to the lighthouse before lunch. We followed that by selecting one of the eating places by the water and had the kind of pleasant and sociable lunch that can make other pursuits just seem like too much effort.

Crete is famous for the Samaria Gorge, perhaps the longest one in Europe. However, it is far from the only one the island has. If you Google "Gorges in Crete" you will find a vast number. I have never walked the Samaria Gorge but I gather it`s as crowded as Bond Street on a Saturday afternoon. It`s 18 km long and is likely to take even a fit walker around five hours, far longer if you stroll. It was one of the excursions available to us on this trip but none of us went for it, perhaps because it involved a start at 5 in the morning. We did however take the shorter walk through the Imbros Gorge which is quite near to Chania.

Before leaving this part of Crete however I decided that one trip I did want to make was the sea crossing to Santorini. This deserves a chapter to itself.

SANTORINI

For a long time I had wanted to visit the island of
Santorini. Every calendar of Greek islands includes a scene
of the white monasteries with blue domes. They sit high
on charred rock with a deep blue sea far below. Some
show the white houses of the town a little downhill from
the domes. Often these white walls in photographs I`ve
seen glow a little from the sunlight as if incandescent. It is
the farthest south of the islands of the Greek Cyclades
group and sits in the sea about 120 miles south-east of
mainland Greece. It has a total land area of about 28
square miles and has a population of around 15,000
people. Of course its hold on the imagination arises from
more than its undeniable scenic drama and beauty. It has
history of the utmost interest. However, before coming to
that unique story it is singular in other ways. The modern
island has agriculture and its volcanic soil provides special
characteristics. Santorini produces tomatoes of unusual
sweetness and flavour. It also has a white aubergine
unlike any found elsewhere, one so tasty it can be eaten
and enjoyed uncooked. The dry white wine from the
Assyrtiko grape is unique and along with it is a prized
sweet dessert wine called Vinsanto. Wine production is
not easy on this island. The volcanic soil only permits

harvests at about 20% of the level in France. However, there is considerable compensation for that in the fact that the Assyrtiko is entirely resistant to the phylloxera pest which has blighted other major wine areas both in the New and the Old world.

So, Santorini would be worth visiting even if there was nothing more to its story. However, there is very much more. A hint of that is found in the various names by which it has been known. From ancient times in Greek it was known as Thera and was often referred to as Strongili which is Greek for `the round one`. The name, Santorini, comes from the annexation of the island by west Europeans (possibly Franks or Italians) during the crusades. They named it after Saint Irene `Santo Irini`. This in itself is rather ironic since the name Irene is Greek for `peace`. This island has often been far from peaceful. The name Strongili seems very strange if you look at a map. The island is not at all round. It is more in the shape of a crescent with a couple of islets beside it. This would be a clue, if you did not already know, that something strange has happened here. That `strange` thing was of course the largest volcanic explosion in recorded history. Carbon dating and tree ring evidence suggest the most likely date for the major part of this cataclysm was around 1625 BC. This is further corroborated by reports such as crop failure in China around that time. It is certain that such a gigantic explosion would have affected climate far beyond the immediate area. The eruption took away the central and western parts of the island and left a lagoon which measures about 12 miles by 7.5. The remaining cliffs at what must have been the edge of the explosion rise to around 1,000 feet (300 metres) and the lagoon has a depth of around 1200 feet (400 metres). This gives some idea of the immense amount of rock which was blown into the sky above the Aegean in that event, a quantity estimated at 15 cubic miles in volume. Along with the molten rock, lava and pyroclastic clouds emanating from the earth came a gigantic tsunami that certainly reached Crete and perhaps far beyond.

This immense disaster obviously destroyed life on the island itself. However, it is quite likely that it or its immediate aftermath also largely destroyed the highly developed Minoan civilisation of Crete. Furthermore, it is very probable that it left its mark on ancient writings. The geologist, Barbara Sivertsen and the filmaker, Simcha Jacobovici amongst others have put forward the view that this cataclysm explains phenomena in the Bible such as the flood, the parting of the Red Sea and the plagues of Egypt. A number of scholars have found close parallels with Plato's description of Atlantis and its disappearance.

Understandably the island then remained uninhabited for a long time, but was eventually resettled despite the fact that it sits in what is probably the world's most active earthquake zone and further eruptions have caused more damage, notably a serious one in 1956. As with much of Greece and neighbouring countries, as with San Francisco, the inhabitants must simply live with the knowledge that their lives and livelihoods could be destroyed at any moment. It is surprising what dangers humans will sometimes accept.

So, for a number of years I had harboured the intention to visit Santorini one day, but it is not particularly accessible. However, on my last visit to Crete I noticed that there was an excursion to it available if I didn`t mind getting up at five in the morning and missing breakfast. No one else in the group I had joined at lolida near Chania was tempted so I trudged out alone in the dark early morning to await the bus that would take us to the harbour at Rethymnon from which the boat was to leave. The bored night porter who was always amused by my sallies into her native language gladly made me a decent cup of coffee as we chatted for the few minutes before the coach pulled up to take me on my way. It was a comfortable, warm bus and I settled down, knowing I had about an hour and a half during which I could catch up on some sleep.

The ferry at Rethymnion was one of these huge craft which takes cars, buses, trucks and countless humans. I made my way on accompanied by large numbers, mostly, I came to realise, Russians. Again I slept on one of the comfortably upholstered seats in the lounge area for much of the crossing. I was not alone as I realised on waking with snoring, dozing bodies draped over much of the furniture. I went on deck and eventually began to see fragments of rock in the sea. One particularly took my attention. It closely resembled a boat with a bearded man standing on it with a pole. I had to look at it repeatedly as we approached it to be sure that was not what it was. Soon the much larger mass of Santorini began to rise above the horizon. I was surprised at the thrill this gave me. I was witnessing a survivor of perhaps the greatest cataclysm of the last few thousand years and perhaps longer. It seemed to demand a special reverence. Many of us gathered on deck to watch the mighty relic, others perhaps aware as I was that we were crossing the caldera of history`s greatest volcano. As we moved closer and closer over the intensely blue sea I began to realise that I would have to revise my plans. I had thought that on disembarkation I would simply walk up to Fira and enjoy the view as I climbed. However, I had been basing this on the old landing place of Fira Skala, just round the coast, from which you could walk or hire a donkey. I began to realise we were heading for the new docking area at Athinios which was wide enough to hold a large number of tour buses and service buses. However, from what I could see, strolling up to Fira was not an option. With crampons and several years survival training with special forces I could possibly manage, but the only serious option appeared to be a bus. As the giant doors of the huge ferry opened my fellow passengers roared off as if jet-propelled, heading unerringly for one or other of the many coaches. I found myself wandering almost alone from bus to bus realising that any I could see were forbidden to me as I was not a member of any group. Fortunately there were a number of cafés at the far end of this area, at the foot of the charred cliff. I asked one of the waiters what the secret was of reaching Fira. He smiled as if he dealt with this question during most of his working day. He pointed to two of the buses in the vast array and advised that they were the service buses for Fira. He thought the one on the left the more likely to leave first. I thanked him and went over to the indicated coach whose driver pointed to the other as I approached. I went to the other one and the exasperated driver turned to the first one and shouted something at him which I could not catch but was clearly offensive. The first driver shrugged and yelled back with hand gestures that suggested his life was an intolerable burden already and that taking me as a passenger was more than human strength could take. I put aside my understandable feelings of being unloved and unwanted and decided to explain in as near as I could get to flawless Greek that I was a hapless Scotsman who had for years yearned to reach Santorini and now that I had done so I could not in all conscience be abandoned. This appeared to silence both drivers who stared at me as if I were a new life form. The first driver nodded for a moment and then with a resigned hand gesture invited me aboard. He already had about ten passengers so why I had posed such a problem I`ll never know.

It was a short walk from the bus station up to the town centre and I found that a remarkable experience. Going in amongst the brilliantly white buildings of Fira was like entering an ice-cream city, except that the temperature was already far more than any ice cream could ever have tolerated. I walked up the hill past a colonnade of pure white stone beside a white tower. Then I turned left at the top of the hill. Immediately I was on a road designed for style, luxury, expense. Louis Vuitton, Armani, Bulgari and others all called to the wealthy tourists. I passed a café on my left which seemed to encapsulate the town of Fira. It was a short way down the slope and you could easily look over it to the intense blue sea far below and the smaller island of Nea Kamini in the lagoon. In the café itself shade was provided from the hot sun by a series of pink-topped parasols like giant flowers. Below them the seating areas were divided off by low, white walls. The tables were round and bronze and at each were two upholstered seats like mini-sofas, all with blue and pink stripes. You could regard it as pretentious but in fact I thought it beautiful, designed with exquisite taste. I didn`t stop at this one although it was near coffee-time as far as I could tell. My system was a little disorientated from the early rise and, perhaps, from the unexpected Russian elbowing. A few yards further on I did go into one which was less of a work of art but was nonetheless modern and tasteful. I was able to take a seat in partial shade looking down towards the intensely blue sea below me.

As I waited for service I picked up a local paper and read about some of the island's personalities. It was the Santorini News and a journalist called Dmitry Prasso was writing about the airport. A waiter approached and I ordered coffee. When he returned he expressed some surprise that I was reading the paper. We chatted and I discovered he was not a native of the island. He originally came from Hydra and intended to return there to take over his father's business at some stage. In the meantime he wanted to know more of Greece. He loved Santorini but he thought there was something unreal about it that disqualified it as a long-term home. I already had some idea what he meant. He suggested that if I was interested there was a small museum in Mitropoleos street near the town centre where there were finds about the ancient history of the island when it was still round and deserved the name, Stroggoli. I thanked him and enjoyed my coffee, looking out at the mesmerisingly azure sea. Some of the sense of unreality mentioned by the waiter arose, I felt, from the intensity of that blue. Perhaps this came partly from the depth of the caldera in which it sat. Perhaps it was simply the contrast with the white buildings of Fira or the effect of the intense sunlight. Maybe it was the altitude from which I was viewing it. Perhaps I had simply seen it too often in calendars to accept it as a real place. Maybe all of these combined to give me a sense that it could all fade away or, perhaps more accurately, that it was not part of the earth at all but a window into another, more poetic reality, a window that might shut at any moment.

After coffee I strolled along the town's main street, Erythrou Stavrou. It was hard to resist the feeling that I was Santorini's most impoverished visitor. Everywhere I looked I saw stylish clothes and cameras that NASA might have envied. Of course the exception to this was the frequent views down the cliff-face to the blue sea and the reminder that the power of nature can overwhelm anything man-made. I had walked through most of the town in the increasing heat when I finally reached a blue-topped church. The photographs I had seen before my visit had suggested the island was covered in them, but not so. On the way I passed an opening with dozens of brilliantly white steps leading up to a church that did not appear to be blue-domed. However, just over halfway up were a newly married couple with the bride's white dress blending with the background, a beautiful sight.

The heat was becoming oppressive and, for the first time, I weakened and bought one of the frozen yoghourts on sale in most of the Greek islands. I chose a pistachio flavour and found a step in the shade where I could sit and enjoy it. This was no small achievement since most shaded seats were already occupied by others reluctant to fry in the middday sun. At least I had my hat made of Chinese plastic which, from a distance, resembled a straw one. I found myself wondering at what temperature Chinese plastic melts and drips down the owner's hair. Fortunately I did not discover this.

I found that escaping from the heat was beginning to take priority in my mind over experiencing Santorini. This seemed like the right time to seek out the museum which would be likely to fulfil both aims. It was easy to find since it was only a few steps away from the bus station where I had arrived. The museum is small but well worth a visit. Most of it is devoted to artefacts excavated at Akrotiri in the south-east of the island. The excavations there were begun in 1967 and proceed slowly. However, what has been discovered is already fascinating. Akrotiri seems to have been one of the most important trading centres in the Aegean from around 2,000 years before Christ to the explosion of the 17th century B.C. It covered an extensive area and had an effective drainage system, multi-storey buildings and extensive wall paintings of a high order. Many of the artefacts discovered show evidence of active trade with other Greek islands as well as Egypt and Turkey. No skeletons have been found at the site. This, along with other evidence, suggests that the inhabitants probably left in an orderly manner before the major eruption. Whether they went far enough to avoid the effects of the mighty cataclysm we cannot of course know. It does however seem as if a large amount of information will come from the excavations since, like Pompeii in Italy, Akrotiri was covered with huge amounts of volcanic ash, thus preserving and protecting what it covered. It is quite possible that some of these fugitives from the volcano went quite far. The story of Atlantis mentioned by Plato in his dialogues *Timaeus* and *Critias* may have resulted from the great philosopher`s ancestor Solon who apparently heard the legend of Atlantis when he was in Egypt. In that version, recounted in *Critias*, the scene of the disaster was in the Delta of the Nile. Whilst Santorini is not in the Delta of the Nile there can be little doubt that the explosion would have impacted upon land and sea in that area. Otherwise, perhaps he heard the story from descendants of those who had left Akrotiri. Plato lived on mainland Greece and later in Italy so they must have travelled quite far if his account is other than hearsay. As I`ve often felt when seeing what remains of the ancient classical world, the standard of workmanship and creativity was very high indeed. These were people who valued art, life and colour. They traded energetically and enjoyed food, drink and nice things, perhaps not very different from the tourists I had come across in modern Fira. Whole murals have been preserved giving more insight into daily life.

I emerged from the museum and was soon uncomfortable again in the powerful sun. I decided it was almost late enough to justify lunch. I went back up to the main street and found another cool, shaded eating place with a view down the cliff. As I sat I reflected that I appeared already to have looked at almost everything this small town had to offer but could not escape from the island for another four hours. This problem had not occurred to me before arriving. I knew now that there was much more to the island than I could see in a day, but to do so would involve either bus journeys or hiring a car to see any of the many beaches or the wines at Pyrgos or the excavations at Akrotiri. In terms of distance it would not have been out of the question to reach one of the neighbouring villages from which there would have been more startling views, but I had no appetite for spending so long in the hot sun. I realised that you have to come to Santorini for either more or less time than I had allotted.

I prolonged lunch as much as possible and then felt irritated with myself. I had wanted for so many years to visit this unique island and here I was with a couple of hours left and no idea what to do with it other than avoid being fried. I decided to walk a little more around the small town, looking for more memorable views to store in my camera. The plan involved seeking shade whenever possible. It was something of an anti-climax, but once I had made this decision I took more time to savour the views and reflect on why this combination of the milk-white buildings, the deeply scarred and blackened cliff and the great expanse of blue sea was so impressive. As the time for my bus approached and I again felt the heat oppressive I decided it would be wise to find shade, a coffee and something else to eat since the return journey would be another three hours plus bus trip. There was an attractive small café just a short walk uphill from the bus station. I sat outside but in pleasant shade and enjoyed a good coffee and one of the spinach pies so widely available in Greece and so enjoyable. I hoped this would fortify me for more assaults from the steel-tipped elbows of Russian travellers.

Feeling more comfortable in the shade and pleased that I had finally reached Santorini my mind began to dwell on connections with my native land. So, you might think that any connection with Scotland will have to be contrived just to show off what a globe-trotting superstar I am. After all, this trip took me to the scene of probably the largest volcanic eruption in recorded history. I, however, live in Scotland where volcanic and seismic activity is almost unheard of. There is a town called Comrie in

Scotland which is known as "Shaky toun" because it experiences more earthquakes than anywhere else in the UK. So, there are days in Comrie where you don`t have to stir your tea since seismic action will do that for you. You are unlikely to suffer any distress from these movements. However, they warranted serious attention in the 19th century and, in 1841, a Committee for the Investigation of Scottish and Irish Earthquakes sprang up and invented the word seismometer. The committee discovered how to evaluate the Epicentre (a point on the Earth's surface where the shock is greatest) and Prof J.D.Forbes designed the first seismometer using an inverted pendulum writing onto a concave disk above. In 1874 the Earthquake House was built near the town on solid rock to hold the Mallet seismometer. I believe there are plans to restore it.

As I looked at the sheer cliff down from Fira at the scorched and blackened rock, like a gigantic overfired biscuit, I thought of this development from the tiny tremors in Scotland. Now much more sophisticated versions of that first seismometer record the restlessness of Greek islands. I also thought of the Scottish polymath, James Hutton, who first observed amongst Scotland`s inert rocks that there must have been times of violent activity from the heat of the earth that pushed through sedimentary rock. I wondered if the immensely gifted people of the eastern Mediterranean in these distant times had devised seismometers of their own to try to understand the terrible distortions of their islands. In 1788 Hutton published his Theory of Earth which effectively founded the science of geology. Naturally, he was widely condemned and vilified for not agreeing that Jehovah threw the universe together in a few days. Like his great contemporaries of the Scottish enlightenment, David Hume and Adam Smith, the Scottish establishment did what it could to silence him. I`m sure the ancient Minoans of Crete and Santorini would have been immensely grateful for anything he could have told them about seismology although, alas, even he could not have done much to save them from disaster.

I made my way the short distance down to the bus station. It is an area large enough for around twenty buses serving all parts of the island. At the lower end of it is a booth or kiosk where an official sits to provide accurate information to travellers. I arrived with, I thought, around fifteen minutes to spare. I decided to check with the official, an exasperated looking man having a fraught conversation with a French couple in English which none of them spoke very well at all. I examined the timetable posted on the wall of the booth. This seemed to confirm when the bus would leave but was not very clear about which one it would be. The French couple moved away, their body language suggesting total failure to obtain the required information. I felt I ought to do better by speaking Greek. I approached the fellow whose expression suggested he wondered where a good eruption was when you needed one. I asked him in Greek which bus would be leaving for Athinios since none of them seemed to have that name on the front. His irritation seemed to grow further and he frowned. "Athinios?" he barked. I nodded. "It went twenty minutes" he said. I couldn't believe this. This not only contradicted the timetable but the instructions we had received on the ferry. I asked him in Greek if he was saying it had left twenty minutes ago. This appeared to exasperate him further and he repeated in his version of English "It went twenty minutes". I was not to be deterred. I asked him to tell me in Greek if the bus for Athinios had left twenty minutes ago. He pointed to his watch and again in English said "Twenty minutes. Twenty minutes." This did not help. Whether he was telling me it had left twenty minutes ago or would leave in twenty minutes the timetable was nonsense and I had a problem. Help arrived in the form of a stout young woman with blond curls and glasses. Evidently she was taking over as the fount of knowledge. I reflected that if the Delphic Oracle had been as helpful then the collapse of Greek civilisation had been inevitable. The exasperated man spoke to her in rapid Greek which I could not understand but I had no doubt he was explaining I was a foreign idiot who couldn't understand English or tell the time. She looked at me with some concern. I explained that I was hoping to take a bus for Athinios but did not know which one and I was concerned since her colleague appeared to be telling me I had missed it. She smiled and explained slowly and carefully in Greek that her colleague had meant it would be leaving in about twenty minutes, now down to fifteen. I pointed out that this seemed to contradict the timetable on the wall. She agreed and explained it was out of date and should have been replaced. I asked which bus it would be. She told me it would be one of two buses over on the right and I should ask the drivers. I was relieved and grateful and recognised that her exasperated colleague simply had a poor grasp of the tenses of the English language. As far as he was concerned "it went" and "it will go" were entirely interchangeable. However, I was not amused to learn I was to go through the same Laurel and Hardy routine with two drivers, neither of whom wanted to take me. As it happened, only one of the buses had a driver as the time approached and he confirmed he was going downhill to the ferry.

It was with some relief that I boarded and settled in one of the comfortable seats. I was very glad finally to have seen Santorini, but have to view it simply as an overture to a much more thorough visit. Since I have taken this decision about many parts of Greece, not to mention other parts of the world, I do hope to be spared for another hundred years.

158

THE END

Robert's gutter
= 1.9 cm
but only 157 pp

CPSIA information can be obtained at www.ICGtesting.com
Printed in the USA
LVOW07s2054140615

442423LV00006BB/909/P